MORE TALES
FROM THE
EAST RIDING

MORE TALES
FROM THE
EAST RIDING

MARTIN LIMON

Martin Limon

TEMPUS

First published 2008

Tempus Publishing
The History Press Ltd.
Cirencester Road, Chalford,
Stroud, Gloucestershire, GL6 8PE
www.thehistorypress.co.uk

Tempus Publishing is an imprint of The History Press Ltd.

British Library Cataloguing in Publication Data.
A catalogue record for this book is available from the British Library.

ISBN 978 0 7524 4753 7

Typesetting and origination by The History Press Ltd.
Printed in Great Britain

Contents

Acknowledgements

In preparing these local history features for publication I would like to give special thanks to the following people and organisations: the staff of the East Riding Archives Service/Local Studies Library, the East Riding Museums Service, the Hull Local Studies Library, the Guildhall Collection of Hull Museums, the Withernsea Lighthouse Museum, the Hedon Museum, Alan Hardy, Paul Lakin, Don Brockway, Les Fisher, Ian Stewart, Penny Stewart, Liam Garrigan, Reckitt Benckiser Ltd, Bill Kenwright Ltd, ITV Productions/Yorkshire Television, the Royal Theatre, Windsor.

In researching the material for this new book and in finding the images to accompany it I would like to thank the numerous individuals who responded to my emails and telephone calls. Thanks also go to Cate Ludlow of The History Press Ltd for her constant encouragement and enthusiasm when I emailed her each new chapter as the book slowly took shape.

I am also grateful to my sons Marc and Tim for their helpful advice and to my wife Lynne for her patience and support during both the research and writing phases of the project.

Introduction

A lot can happen in twelve months, for when *Tales from the East Riding* was published by Tempus in November 2006 I had not really given much thought to a sequel. However, when, during an interview on Radio Humberside, I was asked about my future writing plans I realised that there were many more fascinating local stories to investigate.

As with *Tales from the East Riding* some of the features in this new book have appeared previously in local magazines. One chapter, 'Of Unsound Mind', is based on an article I wrote for *Around the Wolds* magazine as long ago as April 2005. Other features and themes are more recent having appeared in *Yorkshire Ridings Magazine* and the 'village visit' series in the *Journal*, although I have taken the opportunity to include some 'extended' versions for *More Tales from the East Riding*. Other chapters in the book are new and have never before appeared in print.

Martin Limon,
Thearne, Beverley,
East Yorkshire
December 2007

I

Across the Humber

The River Humber has long played an important part of the history of East Yorkshire for this maritime route into the heart of northern England helped to stimulate trade and the growth of ports like Hull and Goole. However, the river that forms the southern boundary of East Yorkshire has also been a barrier to communication and remained so until the opening of the Humber Bridge in June 1981…

With a length of over 64km and an average width of 4.3km, the River Humber has always been a formidable obstacle to the movement of people and goods. The first-known ferry existed in Roman times to link Winteringham with Petuaria (modern-day Brough) and formed part of Ermine Street joining Lincoln and York. Brough was a logical place for a ferry crossing since its haven provided a safe anchorage for ships.

It is clear that the importance of Brough did not end with the departure of the Romans for Brough Ferry was often mentioned in the Middle Ages. An early nineteenth-century history of the village records that: 'The ferry at Brough is still much used for the conveyance of passengers, horses, etc to and from Winteringham.'

At the heart of old Brough was the Ferry Inn dating back to seventeenth century where ferry passengers could obtain refreshments to fortify themselves for the occasionally stormy crossing. Of even greater significance to Brough was the arrival of the railway on 1 July 1840 when the Hull & Selby line opened. Coinciding with the opening of Brough railway station came the introduction of a steam ferry on the Brough crossing and the rebuilding of the Ferry Boat Inn (1841). Yet despite these improvements by the late nineteenth century the Brough Ferry had ceased to operate.

It was the growing dominance of Hull and its role as the hub of railway development that helped bring an end to the multitude of ferry services across the Humber from earlier times. Before the coming of railways, however, the shortest route across the Humber was often preferable and this was provided by another ancient ferry: that from Hessle to Barton. Such was the ferry's importance in the eighteenth century that the road from Hessle to Beverley was improved by the creation of a turnpike trust in April 1769.

Barton was also a destination of ferries operating from Hull and by the late eighteenth century landing stages and a coaching inn had been provided for the convenience of travellers. The crossing, however, was not always pleasant, and the writer Daniel Defoe reported on the discomforts of it when he wrote:

Barton is a town noted for nothing that I know of but an ill-favoured dangerous passage or ferry over the Humber to Hull. In an open boat in which we had about fifteen horses and ten or twelve cows mingled with about seventeen or eighteen passengers we were about four hours tossed about on the Humber before we could get into the harbour at Hull.

Annoyed by both seasickness and by the delay Defoe decided not to return by the same route!

In 1796 Hull Corporation bought the ferry rights of the Hull to Barton route for £3,000 and in 1821 it leased them to the company that operated the stagecoach service between Barton and

This pub sign of the Ferry Inn at Brough depicts the kind of Roman ferry that may have once linked Petuaria with Winteringham.

London. It was they who replaced the sailing ships with steam-driven vessels like the *Waterloo* and the *Royal Charter* with four crossings each day.

By about 1826 however the Hull to Barton ferry faced competition from an upstart rival operating between Hull and New Holland. Although it began with simply a rowing boat, by 1832 a steamboat called *Magna Carta* was operating a thrice-daily service. With the transfer of the London mails to the New Holland route in 1836 and the purchase of both ferries by a railway company rationalisation of the ferry crossings became inevitable and by 1851 the Hull to Barton service had ceased to operate.

With the arrival of the railway at New Holland in 1848, the opening of a jetty into the Humber to allow for the transfer of passengers and goods from train to ferry and investment in new paddle steamers the New Holland to Hull service continued for over 100 years. The first paddle steamer built for the railway-to-ferry service was the *Manchester* in 1849 and in the decades that followed a succession of new ferry craft appeared. Three of the most famous in the later history of the Humber Ferries were the *Wingfield Castle* and the *Tattersall Castle* (operating from 1934) and the *Lincoln Castle* (put into service in 1940).

In theory a ferry crossing on the Hull to New Holland route could take as little as twenty minutes, but factors such as fog or other bad weather and shifting sandbanks could cause serious delays. There were other mishaps too and a report in the *Hull Times* of 17 September 1864 recorded a 'frightful occurrence' when a bull broke free and ran amok among the passengers. Three of them, from the Hessle Road area of Hull, were gored before the animal could be brought under control. The newspaper suggested that the Manchester, Sheffield & Lincolnshire Railway ought to provide a separate boat for animals in view of the annoyance caused to passengers by cargoes of horses and cattle.

The delays and inconvenience of the ferry meant that schemes to bridge the river or tunnel under it received considerable local press coverage from 1865 onwards. Some schemes centred on the

The paddle steamer *Lincoln Castle* arriving at New Holland during the final year of the Humber Ferry Service (1981).

desire of Hull merchants to break the monopoly of the North Eastern Railway in the Hull area. In 1872, for example, a proposal for a Hull South & West Junction Railway was launched and included ambitious plans for a tunnel from Hessle to Barton. Unfortunately the House of Lords, partly on engineering grounds, rejected the bill.

An editorial in the *Hull Times* of 10 February 1883 provides some indication of the debate on how a crossing of the Humber might best be achieved when it said:

> *The battle of bridge versus tunnel is still going on and we may expect the contest to be a very sharp one. There are so many reasons in favour of the bridge I wonder why the Manchester, Sheffield and Lincolnshire Railway Company are expending £10,000 to sink borings into the river.*

In fact, plans for a railway bridge across the Humber (by the Hull & Lincoln Railway) were just as unsuccessful; they aroused opposition from the vested interests of existing railway companies and from the port of Goole, which claimed that a multi-spanned bridge would interfere with its rights of navigation.

Thus the debate on a bridge or tunnel crossing – or even if there should be a crossing at all – dragged on into the twentieth century. In May 1924 the minister of transport, Harry Gosling MP, told a group of Hull businessmen that the government could not act until the responsible local authorities had formulated 'some definite project for our consideration' and were prepared to meet some of the cost.

In March 1930, therefore, a committee representing Hull Corporation, East Riding County Council and Lindsey County Council considered a report of the engineers Sir Douglas Fox & Partners on the relative merits of tunnels and bridges. The report suggested that a road tunnel would cost £7.2 million but that a road bridge could be built for £1.725 million. The engineers suggested

Artist's impression from the 1930s depicting how the multi-span steel-trussed road bridge across the Humber may have looked if it had been built then.

that any tunnel would be prohibitively expensive and that the best option was a steel-trussed multi-span road bridge.

Yet, progress was delayed by the issue of finance. In June 1930 Hull Corporation announced that they were prepared to pay £200,000 towards the cost of a bridge on the condition that the rest of the money was found by central government and other interested local councils. Hull councillor Benno Pearlman suggested that the East Riding County Council and Lindsey County Council should follow Hull's lead by contributing £50,000 each. It was optimistically suggested that the bridge might attract government money in order to relieve unemployment. However, the East Riding County Council was less enthusiastic and more prudent. Lord Deramore (the council chairman) said that he 'could not hold out any hope of a contribution from the County Council' and indicated the tensions between the two local authorities by claiming:

> There was a feeling in the East Riding that they were heavily rated maintaining roads for the benefit of Hull. Heavy transports coming from the West Riding to Hull were a tremendous burden on the East Riding who obtained no benefit at all from that prosperity.

In the event the East Riding County Council refused to make a financial commitment to the scheme and as the 'great depression' of the 1930s took hold, central government too became more cautious. When in February 1934 local MP Louis Smith asked in the House of Commons if the government was prepared to give any assistance for a bridge or a tunnel he was told that it could not 'in the present financial circumstances.'

The Humber Bridge therefore remained a project on the drawing board and it was here that real progress was made in the 1930s. The civil engineer Sir Ralph Freeman (1880-1950), inspired by the building of San Francisco's Golden Gate Bridge from 1933, proposed a suspension bridge for the Humber (1935). It was this idea that was to bear fruit when construction finally began in 1972.

The Humber Bridge Board Act of 1959 established a bridge authority to build a single-span suspension bridge between Hessle and Barton and collect tolls but it required both political will and finance for the work to start. When the go-ahead for this massive civil-engineering project was given, the decision was due more to politics than to need. In January 1966 there was a by-election in the constituency of Hull North. Harold Wilson's Labour Government had a tiny majority in the House of Commons and required a victory in the Hull North by-election as a springboard for a General Election campaign. The minister for transport, Barbara Castle, was thus persuaded to give the Humber Bridge her approval in order to produce the required Labour victory in North Hull and triumph in the General Election that followed it. Her announcement did both and the decision to commence work was duly made three years later.

The Humber Bridge from the Lincolnshire side of the river. Slip-formed concrete rather than steel was a feature of the towers. However, problems with the foundations of the south tower added to the cost of the bridge and delayed its completion until 1981.

The building of the bridge was a mammoth undertaking and took nine years to complete. Problems with the foundations of the south tower added to the cost of the structure and delayed its completion. The £55 million needed to finish the project however did finally provide a way of crossing the river less susceptible to disruption and delay than the Humber ferries. For local traffic the bridge meant much-reduced journeys with, for example, the trip from Hull to Grimsby being forty-eight miles shorter than the alternative of 'going round by Goole'. Yet, the huge debts built up both during and since construction now stand at over £300 million and the tolls charged (currently £2.70 each way for a car crossing) make the Humber Bridge the most expensive toll crossing in Britain.

The official opening of the bridge by the Queen on 17 July 1981 was the realisation of a dream that had begun over a century earlier. One immediate effect was the end of the Humber Ferry Service from Hull to New Holland with the last run being performed by the diesel-electric paddle steamer *Farringford* on the 24 June 1981 (the day the bridge first opened to traffic). A quarter of a century after it opened the Humber Bridge, its tolls and its debt remain controversial political issues.

Dubbed by some as 'the bridge to nowhere' and an 'irrelevance' to Britain's motorway network, there is no doubt that the Humber crossing was at a disadvantage from the moment of its birth. Other estuarial road bridges like the Forth Bridge (opened 1964) and the Severn Bridge (opened 1966) cost much less to build and were not saddled with the same level of debt as the Humber Bridge (built in the inflationary 1970s). In addition the Forth Bridge and the Severn Bridge are part of busy major routes serving Scotland and Wales whereas the Humber Bridge still awaits its role as a link in a possible east-coast motorway.

2

Sir Cornelius Vermuyden and
the Dutch Connection

While many settlements in East Yorkshire can claim to be the oldest in the county, among the 'newest' places is the port of Goole; a directory of 1837 said that it had 'sprung into existence during the last fifteen years'. Modern Goole owed its rapid growth to the building of the Knottingley and Goole Canal (completed in 1826) although the origins of Old Goole were much older. They date back to the seventeenth century with the digging of the 'Dutch River' by the great Dutch engineer Cornelius Vermuyden…

It is difficult to imagine a time when Britain's landscape looked very different from the neat 'patchwork quilt' of fields of today. However, 500 years ago large parts of the countryside in the eastern counties lay under water and played little part in the agrarian economy of the time. In Tudor England places like the Isle of Axholme and Hatfield Chase, two extensive marshes in North Nottinghamshire, Lincolnshire and South West Yorkshire, covered an area of 70,000 acres and were of little value other than for fishing or wildfowling.

As early as the reign of Elizabeth I it had been suggested that this extensive marshland should be drained, but nothing was done. It was left to her successor, James I, to make a start on the project. In 1621 James had made contact with the Dutch drainage engineer, Cornelius Vermuyden, after the Thames had overflowed its banks. It was natural that the shrewd Stuart King should look to the Netherlands for this kind of expertise, for the people of the Low Countries possessed a long experience of keeping water under control by draining lakes, pools and marshes.

Cornelius Vermuyden had been born on the island of Tholen in the province of Zeeland in 1595 and by the time of his arrival in England had taught himself something about land reclamation, improved drainage and building river embankments. In 1626 the new King, Charles I made an agreement with Vermuyden to drain Hatfield Chase in the Isle of Axholme. The newly drained land would then be divided into three parts with the Crown, Vermuyden and the existing tenants each receiving a share.

The work was funded by the sale of Vermuyden's land to a number of partners called 'participants', many of whom were Dutch or Flemish. Vermuyden also recruited an army of his fellow countrymen to do the actual work of digging ditches and building embankments using only the most primitive of tools.

Much of their endeavours involved the redirection of the waters of the River Don for these, in the sixteenth century, meandered slowly in a northeasterly direction across the marshes of Hatfield Chase and into the River Trent. One branch of the Don flowed into a lake or mere situated between Stainforth and Thorne and by severing this and building a network of drains and dykes the mere was drained. Another part of Vermuyden's schemes, in the early 1630s, was to cut a broad canal to carry the waters of the Don from New Bridge eastwards in a straight line to the River Ouse instead of the River Trent. This canal became known as the 'Dutch River' and with its high embankments and its sluice gates defending the outfalls from the drains of Hatfield Chase represented a considerable engineering achievement for the seventeenth century. It was at the junction of the Dutch River and the River Ouse that the tiny hamlet of Old Goole was to slowly develop over succeeding centuries (although by 1831 it still only had a population of 400 people).

Sir Cornelius Vermuyden (1590–1677) from a
contemporary portrait.

Yet the work of draining Hatfield Chase was not without its problems for many of the local inhabitants resented the newcomers who, by draining the marshes, had come to 'deprive' them of their traditional rights to take wildfowl and fish the pools and rivers.

The settlement of the newly reclaimed lands by hundreds of settlers from the Dutch Netherlands, Flanders and by French Huguenots escaping religious persecution were a further source of grievance. The breakdown of law and order with the coming of the English Civil War in 1642 was to give the local inhabitants the chance to strike back. In June 1642 the colonists of Sandtoft, who had built a settlement there with houses and a church and were farming the rich soils of the area, found themselves under attack from the locals who 'arose in tumults, broke down the Fenns and enclosures destroyed all the corn growing and demolished the houses thereon'.

Meanwhile, Cornelius Vermuyden, knighted by Charles I in 1629 for his work on Hatfield Chase, had moved on to an even greater project: draining 300,000 acres of the East Anglian Fens. Until the seventeenth century the Fens were vast tracts of sedge-covered swamp with a few settlements like Ely occupying 'islands' of higher ground. Vermuyden recognised that the solution lay in diverting the waters of the meandering natural rivers into straight artificial cuts. These canals would then carry the excess water of the area to the sea by the shortest route.

The project began in 1634 when a group of adventurers (or financiers) led by the Fourth Earl of Bedford obtained permission to drain the peat part of the Fens, known as the Great Level or Bedford Level, in Cambridgeshire. In return for their investment each of the adventurers was to receive a share of the reclaimed land while Vermuyden would get 95,000 acres. During the 1630s he and his men built nine drainage cuts of between two and twenty-one miles in length. His major work was in constructing the Old Bedford River, twenty-one miles long, completed in 1637 but which later attracted criticism from other engineers who claimed the work was inadequate.

The Dutch workers settled on land owned by the Earl of Bedford at Thorney near Peterborough and were later joined by those fleeing from the ill-fated settlement at Sandtoft. However, in the Fens too their work was soon under attack from the local inhabitants distrustful of the outsiders and angry about the loss of their 'rights'. These opponents to the work of Vermuyden and the adventurers were called 'Fen Tigers' and their sabotage ranged from small-scale, night-time attacks on sluice gates to mass riots with the intent of destroying the drainage works completely. One example was in June 1638 at Whelpmore Fen (Isle of Ely) where a large crowd tried to level the ditches that had been dug. In August 1641, five miles north of Ely, Littleport Sluice was damaged when protesters directed a boat filled with burning straw down the channel and into the gate. Further acts of destruction both by rioters and the military followed during the English Civil War of 1642–1646.

Work resumed on the Great Level after the Civil War when a new Bedford Act was passed by Parliament in May 1649. In 1651 Vermuyden began work on the New Bedford River, a 100ft-wide channel dug parallel to the first, and excavated in malarial conditions by Scottish prisoners of war captured after the Battle of Dunbar (1650). Dutch prisoners were also used to do the work. As before, the local inhabitants showed their resentment through acts of sabotage and there were riots at Swaffham in 1652. Such was the unrest that troops had to be sent to restore order.

However, both during the time of Cromwell and the Restoration that followed the work continued, converting thousands of acres into some of Britain's most productive agricultural land. This was the lasting legacy of Cornelius Vermuyden, even though many criticised his methods both at the time and since. One of the main criticisms laid against him arose over a problem he could not have foreseen: that in time the rich peat through which his channels had been dug began to dry out and the level of the land lowered. During the eighteenth century windmills had to be installed (and in the nineteenth century steam pumps) to lift the water into the drains.

Despite these criticisms of Vermuyden's work there is no denying his considerable achievement in bringing Dutch reclamation methods to Britain and in converting thousands of acres of wetland bogs into rich, productive farmland. By the time of his death in October 1677 Vermuyden's work had transformed large areas of eastern England and had created hundreds of miles of navigable waterways.

His achievement was even more remarkable given the political upheavals of the Civil War period and the violent opposition of local inhabitants. It is testament to Vermuyden's abilities that even when some of his projects did not completely satisfy his customer's expectations they continued to employ him on new ones. Furthermore, his legacy to eastern England lives on centuries after his death through the naming of schools (like Vermuyden School in Goole), roads and businesses.

The Dutch River at Goole from an old postcard.

3

When Civil War Came to East Yorkshire

The 22 August 1642 is often suggested as a landmark date in our history for, it is claimed, the day was the 'start' of the English Civil War. In fact this was merely the occasion that hostilities formally commenced at Nottingham (with the raising of the royal standard to rally the King's supporters to arms) since there had been a state of undeclared war between King and Parliament for several months before. Nowhere was this more apparent than in East Yorkshire…

Years of growing mistrust between King Charles I and his subjects (over issues like illegal taxation) and culminating in the King's attempt to arrest his leading opponents in the House of Commons in January 1642, had already set the country on the road to civil war. The King soon moved his court north to York while his Queen, Henrietta Maria, left England for the Netherlands to pawn the royal jewels in order to buy arms and raise troops.

In these early months of 1642 it was to be the fortified town and port of Hull that was to be a focus of attention for both King and Parliament. The King needed Hull as a means of bringing in supplies from abroad, but more importantly for the arsenal of weapons stored in its ancient manor house. However, the governor of Hull, Sir John Hotham had been given instructions by Parliament not to 'deliver up the town of Hull or magazine without their authority.'

The scene was therefore set for a confrontation and this took place on Saturday 23 April 1642 with the arrival of the King. Forewarned of his coming, Hotham had already met with other key figures in Hull including Peregrine Pelham MP, Henry Barnard (the mayor) and Lt-Col. Christopher Legard, an officer of the newly strengthened Hull garrison. In view of Parliament's orders it was therefore decided to close the gates and raise the drawbridges to deny the King entry to the town. When Charles and his retinue arrived at Hull's Beverley Gate he was unable to persuade Hotham, in four hours of fruitless negotiations, to allow him to enter and, after declaring the governor to be a traitor, the royal party was forced to return to Beverley and thence to York.

By July 1642 the King was back in Beverley setting up his court there and determined to take Hull by force if necessary. The clerk of St Mary's church, Nicholas Pearson, wrote of his arrival in the parish registers: 'King came to town the seventh day. Hull mills burnt the 11th day.'

Setting fire to windmills close to Hull's walls in order to cut off the town's food supply (and to intimidate the defenders) was only part of the Royalist strategy for other troopers were also busy trying to disrupt the water supply from sources west of Hull. In this first siege it has been estimated that a Royalist army of 3,000 foot soldiers and 1,000 horses surrounded Hull from Hessle in the west, through Cottingham to Paull in the east. Had the Royalists been able to move siege cannon into place (or get close enough to undermine the fortifications) then it is clear that Hull's brick walls and gates would not have been able to withstand the onslaught for long. However, Hull was saved by the low-lying terrain and a decision to open the sluices and break down the banks of the Humber in order to create a barrier of flooded land two miles wide. Nor were Hull's defenders passive in their defence of the town; the Royalists had established a base at the manor house in the village of Anlaby, west of Hull, and on 27 July a force from the Hull garrison, using rafts to negotiate the flooded ground,

This triple portrait of Charles I was painted by Anthony van Dyck around 1635. After moving his court to York early in 1642 King Charles I was eager to take control of Hull both for the arsenal of weapons stored in its ancient manor house and as a port to bring in troops and munitions from the continent.

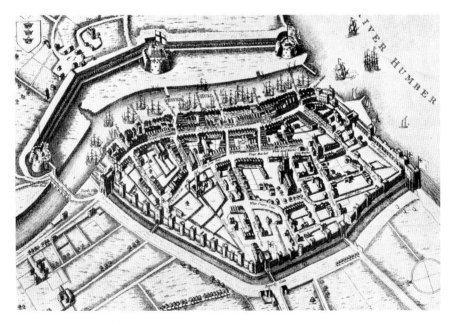

Bird's-eye view of Hull around the year 1640 by Wenceslas Hollar.

launched a surprise night attack on it. The ambush was very successful in taking the Royalist troops unawares; a cache of munitions was destroyed, a dozen or so prisoners captured while other Royalist troops fled in panic. Meanwhile, other reinforcements sent into beleaguered Hull by sea, and under the command of Sir John Meldrum, had attacked Royalist positions on the road to Beverley and seem to have reached the town itself. These skirmishes may have been what Nicholas Pearson was referring to when he wrote on 19 July 1642: 'King's war hot at Beverley.' What is clear is that the attempts of Charles I to capture Hull by siege had failed and he then withdrew. Significantly these military actions around Hull, Anlaby and Beverley resulting in loss of life, injury and the taking of prisoners took place over a month before the 'official start' of the Civil War on 22 August!

With the focus of war shifted elsewhere the Hull garrison was able to sally forth and create havoc in Royalist areas. On 4 October a force led by Capt. Hotham (the son of Sir John) captured Cawood Castle only eight miles from York itself. Beverley too changed hands: without walls and only its 'bars' to protect it the town was quickly occupied by men of the Hull garrison who were billeted on the unfortunate householders.

Yet, the Parliamentarians did not have things all their own way. On 22 February Queen Henrietta Maria returned from the Netherlands landing at Bridlington with purchases of arms and stores after being kept at sea for nine days by violent storms. Worse was to follow; Parliamentary ships commanded by Admiral Batten began a bombardment of the town and she was forced to take refuge in a ditch as 'cannon balls sung merrily over her head.'

The Queen survived the attack however and was able to join the commander of the King's northern army, William Cavendish (the Duke of Newcastle), at York and later move south to be reunited with her husband. The arrival of the Queen also paved the way for negotiations with the Hothams who, alarmed at the way the war was escalating, were making plans to change sides. However, before this could happen, on 28 June 1643 Sir John Hotham's former friends became aware of his treachery. Forced to flee from Hull he made his way to Beverley but was arrested there by Col. Boynton commanding the Parliamentary forces in the town. Hotham's planned defection to the Royalist cause seems to have been the signal for an intended uprising against the Parliamentarians for on the 30 June 1643 Nicholas Pearson reported: 'A great scrimmage in Beverley yesterday. War in our gates. Thirteen slaine men in the King's party was buried the 30th day.'

Yet though the Parliamentarians had succeeded in foiling the plot their success was not to last. Cavalry raids on Royalist strongholds in the East Riding by Sir Thomas Fairfax (using Beverley as his base of operations in July and August 1643) culminated in an attack on Stamford Bridge only eight miles from York. The Duke of Newcastle saw that he would have to deal with this threat before moving south in the direction of London and led his army towards Beverley and Hull in late August 1643. Fairfax realised that Beverley was an 'open place' incapable of effective defence and although he fought a delaying action in the town this was done to enable the bulk of his army to escape south behind the walls of Hull rather than because of any sense of obligation to the inhabitants.

On 28 August Beverley was effectively left to the mercies of a marauding Royalist army who, according to Parliamentary propaganda of the time, 'plundered the whole town consisting of above a thousand families and sent their booty of cattle and goods to York.' Beverley was not the only place to suffer, for Newcastle's forces now laid siege to Hull for a second time. With Royalist troops stationed in villages like Newland, Cottingham and Anlaby the inhabitants suffered all the horrors of occupation by an unpaid army that sought to compensate themselves in other ways. In a letter of 24 October 1643 a bailiff of Cottingham wrote: 'Misery is fallen upon us. Our horses, beasts and sheep are driven away and most of our houses plundered. We are now brought to utter ruin.'

If the depredations of the soldiers were not bad enough Cottingham's residents also had to contend with a mass of women camp-followers who had followed their menfolk to the battle area and robbed the inhabitants 'of all their linen without any pity at all.'

The second siege of Hull began on 2 September 1643. However, the besieging Royalist army of 1643 was about four times the size of the one a year earlier and was much better equipped. The Duke of Newcastle's forces brought with them an artillery train including the huge siege cannon Gog and Magog and, to make them as effective as possible against Hull's defences, firing positions were constructed as close as possible to the walls. One of these was Fort Royal, built near to the Beverley

Portrait of Sir Thomas Fairfax. After his defeat at the Battle of Adwalton Moor in June 1643, Fairfax had retreated with his cavalry to Hull. Using Beverley as a forward base he launched attacks on royalist strongholds in East Yorkshire.

Road in Sculcoates and from which the Royalists attempted to send red-hot shot into the town in order to start fires. The bombardment seems to have had only limited success for it is said that only three civilians died during the second siege of Hull.

With their command of the sea the Parliamentarians were also able to bring in supplies and reinforcements. As with the first siege, Hull's defenders chose to take the fight to their enemies by launching an attack against the village of Anlaby. This time however the Royalists seemed to have been better prepared and the assault was beaten off with at least twenty members of the Hull garrison being killed and others being taken prisoner.

Like the first siege of Hull, the most effective tactic of the defenders was to flood the area around the walls by cutting the Humber riverbanks and opening the sluices (14 Sept 1643). Furthermore, an audacious sally out of the town to the west by its defenders (October 11) succeeded in capturing some of the more dangerous Royalist artillery. As before, the Royalist siege of Hull was a failure and the duke ordered a retreat with his troops carrying out acts of sabotage to forestall any pursuit and stealing valuable plate from Cottingham church.

With the threat to Hull lifted the Parliamentarians were free once more to resume their attacks on Royalist targets in the East Riding. One of these was the former priory at Watton, on the road to Driffield north of Beverley. In late 1643 it was the property of Sir Thomas Earlkyn and was garrisoned by a Royalist force. The Parliamentarians laid siege it from two miles away placing their artillery on Barf Hill to the south.

By January 1644 Lord Newcastle's army had a new threat to deal with. A Scottish army, in alliance with Parliament, had invaded Northumberland and as the duke moved north to confront it Royalist garrisons in East Yorkshire were left vulnerable. A Parliamentary striking force of about 600 cavalry

Unlike Hull, the town of Beverley had no walls, only bars or gateways to defend the principal entrances to the town. Shown here is Newbegin Bar. Charles I used Beverley as a base to lay siege to Hull on two occasions (in July 1642 and September/October 1643). At other times Parliamentary forces occupied it. Newbegin Bar was demolished in the eighteenth century.

and 200 infantry, led by Sir William Constable of Flamborough, swept out into the Riding to mop up pockets of Royalist resistance. By early February Constable, an experienced soldier who had fought at the Battle of Edgehill, attacked and routed about 250 Royalist troops near Bridlington and took the town along with its newly appointed governor, Major Newman. It seems likely that the Battle of Bridlington was only one of a series of actions in which Sir William Constable took possession of the whole East Riding for Parliament.

The Civil War in East Yorkshire thus ended with the failure of two Royalist sieges of Hull and, through the strategic importance of the place, Parliamentary control of the entire county. This victory by the Parliamentarians was achieved in spite of a situation where the natural loyalties of most East Yorkshire folk would probably have been with the King. This was a pattern that was soon to be repeated elsewhere in England with crucial Parliamentary victories at the Battles of Marston Moor (2 July 1644) and Naseby (14 June 1645).

4

A Dark Deed at Long Riston

The Holderness village of Long Rishton, six miles east of Beverley, has a history dating back to Anglo-Saxon times. The latter part of its name is thought to mean the 'farmstead near the brushwood.' One of the most chilling episodes from its past was an infamous case of child murder from the year 1799.

Like many villages in the East Riding since the end of the Second World War, Long Riston has seen much new house building in recent times since its location on the A165 has made it very convenient as a commuter settlement for both Hull and Beverley. Between 1891 and 1991 the population of this 'long and straggling' village (as one nineteenth-century directory described it) had doubled to 527 people. Unlike many other rural settlements, however, Long Riston has not been afflicted by ever-increasing numbers of lorries and cars for in 1986 the village obtained a bypass to take traffic away from its main street. Yet some residents see the bypass as a mixed blessing. Audrey Ashcroft has lived in Long Riston for over thirty years and once owned the village shop. As she points out:

The bypass was good for the village in one way in that it got rid of the traffic but it did take trade away from the place. One of the businesses affected was the village garage which has relocated from the main street to a site on the bypass itself.

Although Long Riston's post office and village shop have closed their doors, its public house, the Travellers Rest, remains an important focal point of the community; the inn was mentioned in a directory of 1823 when William Green was the landlord. In fact Long Riston also had a second, pre-1869 beerhouse called the Board Inn. By 1913, however, a report in the East Riding Archives suggested that that the 'premises were dilapidated and in a very bad condition generally'. Under the Licensing Act of 1904 local councils had the power to close down public houses when new licences were sought. This happened in the case of the Board Inn and its owners, the Hartshorne Brewery of Burton-on-Trent, then sought compensation of £319 16s from the East Riding County Council.

In any village community the church is often the oldest building and Long Riston is no exception. The church of St Margaret stands isolated in fields at the north end of the village and dates back to the twelfth century. In bygone times the church played a more central role and the parish registers of Long Riston provide an important record of the key events in villager's lives: baptism records, banns of marriage and burials. These registers, now held by the East Riding Archives Service in Beverley, also hold important clues to a dastardly murder that took place in the village over 200 years ago.

The Long Riston parish registers show that on 24 July 1796 Thomas Hostler, the son of William Hostler (a labourer) and his wife Mary was baptised. Tragically, when the infant Thomas was only one year and seven months old his mother died. A worse tragedy was soon to follow. Perhaps driven by the need to find someone to care for his son, William Hostler remarried less than two months later. His new wife was called Jane Beal and although we know nothing of her background we do know that she was illiterate since she could not sign the register on the day of her marriage (9 April 1798) and had to have her 'mark' witnessed by someone else.

The twelfth-century church of St Margaret in Long Riston stands isolated at the northern end of the village. Thomas Hostler (aged two), a victim of child murder, was buried here on 11 April 1799.

It would seem that William Hostler made a serious error of judgement in choosing Jane Beal as his bride since subsequent events suggest that she cared little for his infant son. The two-year-old boy died only twelve months after the marriage and was buried on 11 April 1799. Other records in the East Riding Archive show the extent of the child's suffering at the hands of his stepmother for on 16 July William Hostler, Jane Hostler and her sister Elizabeth Beal appeared at the East Riding Assizes in Beverley charged with his murder. Five witnesses (including three from Long Riston) had been bound over to appear at the trial to give evidence and they probably provided the facts on which the charges were based. It was said that the three accused had, between 2 February and 10 April 1799, 'made an assault on Thomas Hostler with their hands and feet and with whips, sticks and staves giving him many wounds especially a large wound on the left side of his head.' The charges went on to say that the three had then neglected to provide the infant with food and medical attention.

With the typical speed of eighteenth-century justice the case took only one day. The foreman of the jury, Mathias Williamson, and the other jurors having retired to consider their verdict found Jane Hostler and Elizabeth Beal guilty of the charges but William Hostler not guilty. The eighteenth-century parchment recording the charges also gave the judgement of the court, almost as an afterthought scribbled into a corner. It was ordered that the two women should be put in the pillory in Beverley Market Place and then conveyed to York Castle for transportation.

The pillory was an instrument of punishment whereby the prisoner had to stand with their head and hands clamped between two wooden boards. The aim of the device was to expose particularly notorious criminals to ridicule (and sometimes to physical assault) by the public. In Beverley the pillory was a moveable structure and from records in the East Riding Archive we know that someone was paid to fix it in the Market Place as and when needed. The two women who had been convicted of the murder of the infant Thomas Hostler would probably have had to endure the taunts and jeers of outraged onlookers for perhaps an hour or two before being taken back to the Beverley

The pillory and the stocks were widely used before the nineteenth century to ensure the public humiliation of criminals. After their conviction Jane Hostler and Elizabeth Beal were placed in the pillory in Beverley Market Place.

House of Correction and thence to York. Changes in the law meant that the use of the pillory as a form of punishment was abolished in 1837.

At the close of the eighteenth century transportation usually meant transportation to one of Australia's penal colonies like Port Jackson in New South Wales. However, we do not know if Jane Hostler or her sister ever reached Australia. Many convicts served out their sentences, or died, in the insanitary prison hulks moored at Deptford on the River Thames while awaiting a passage to New South Wales.

While the parish registers record burials in Long Riston from the seventeenth century onwards, another important piece of evidence from the more recent past has also survived: an undertaker's book. A directory of 1892 records the presence in the village of Richard Carlill, joiner and wheelwright, but he also served as the village undertaker and left a detailed account book of his 'customers' and the manner of their deaths. On 17 April 1879, for example, we learn of the death of William Billaney (aged forty) from an overdose of laudanum and that the cost of his coffin, shroud and other fees came to £4 14s. Laudanum was an opium-based painkiller popular in Victorian times for anything ranging from headaches to tuberculosis and many people used it as a kind of recreational drug and became addicted. However, in the case of William Billaney's death it is unclear whether this was suicide or an accident. More clear cut was an entry of 14 February 1864 marking the sale of a coffin for John Spencer of Riston, who had hanged himself. Equally tragic was the death on Monday 15 September 1913 of William, the four-year-old son of Miss Frances Clark, who was 'accidentally killed by a traction engine.' Traction engines were widely used on farms at that time for tasks like threshing corn. Long Riston, in common with other local villages, was dominated by the needs of farming and seven farmers are listed in a directory of 1892. One of these, Thomas Boyes Jackson, was also a magistrate and a county councillor; he lived up the road from the village at Riston Grange.

Generations of the Carlill family continued to play an important role at Long Riston and their influence can also be seen with reference to culture and sport in the village. A directory of the late nineteenth-century records that Thomas Carlill was the secretary of the Long Riston Reading Room (established 1880) which had twenty members and was also the honorary secretary and treasurer of Long Riston Cricket Club. Although the cricket club no longer exists, other sports have taken its place, notably football and tennis.

Long Riston AFC was first established as long ago as 1932 and thanks to determined fundraising by the Playing Fields Association has secured first-rate facilities in the village. Through the campaigning efforts of residents like John Sherwood and Phil Ashcroft £60,000 was provided by local construction firms while a grant of £110,000 came from the Football Foundation to improve both playing and changing facilities for the village's seven football teams.

Lawn tennis too has been a major success story in the village since 1961 when two grass courts and one hard court were laid out. Julie Taylor and her husband Len moved to Long Riston in 1988 having found a plot of land on the main street for a self-build house project. Len is the chairman of the tennis club while Julie, a teacher at Hornsea School, organises the women's teams. As Julie said:

> *The Long Riston Tennis Club has gone from strength to strength and our new all-weather courts have become a focal point of the community. We play in the Driffield and District Tennis League and matches take us as far as Pocklington, Sledmere and Malton.*

With its thriving village spirit, excellent sporting facilities, a successful and extended primary school and for the last twenty years a traffic-calmed main street (thanks to its bypass) Long Riston has all the ingredients for continued well-being. As Julie Taylor points out: 'Long Riston is a lovely community!'

The Carlill family of Long Riston around 1890. The Carlills were the village joiners and undertakers. The elderly gentleman seated in the centre of the picture is Richard Carlill (died 1899) and to the left of him are his sons Thomas Richard Carlill and William Butler Carlill. (courtesy of the East Riding Museums Service)

5

Mary Wollstonecraft in Georgian Beverley

In the struggle to win greater rights for women the focus of history has often been on twentieth-century heroines like the suffragette Emmeline Pankhurst. However, an earlier, eighteenth-century pioneer of the feminist movement was the internationally famous writer Mary Wollstonecraft, who spent some of her formative years in the Beverley area of East Yorkshire.

It is one of the more cruel facts of life that 'fame' only comes to some people after their death. So it was with Mary Wollstonecraft (1759-1797), a radical intellectual whose book *A Vindication of the Rights of Women* (1792) is these days seen as a milestone in the women's rights movement but who was reviled in earlier times for her unconventional lifestyle. By the standards of her age her pronouncements on the need to educate and liberate women, her denouncement of marriage and her view that women needed political representation were controversial enough. However, it was the revelations about her private life, her love affairs and her illegitimate child by the American author Gilbert Imlay that shocked 'genteel' society and ruined her reputation for a generation.

In the year 1768 however, the more turbulent years of Mary Wollstonecraft's adult life lay in the future. As a nine-year-old child she moved with her family to a farm near Walkington about three miles from Beverley. Her father Edward Wollstonecraft was a London silk weaver and had inherited a modest fortune of about £10,000 from Mary's grandfather. With pretensions to be a gentleman farmer Edward Wollstonecraft had tried, and failed, in his first attempt at farming in Essex before moving to East Yorkshire. Why he moved to Walkington is unclear but his decision may have been influenced by its cheaper farm rents and the business opportunities that Beverley's races and horse fairs provided. Whatever his motives, it is clear that Edward Wollstonecraft was no farmer and after about three years he moved his wife and seven children to a house in Beverley's Wednesday Market in order to live the life of a gentleman.

To an impressionable adolescent girl Beverley must have seemed an attractive, cultured place. Eighteenth-century commentators remarked on the town's handsome houses, broad clean streets, beautiful gardens and its 'sweet and wholesome air'. One of these handsome houses, in Lairgate, was owned by one of Beverley's great patrons, Sir James Pennyman, who at about the time of the Wollstonecraft's arrival began to enlarge it by adding new dining and drawing rooms. Today this grand house, The Hall in Lairgate, remains as a fitting tribute to Georgian elegance and good taste.

Pennyman was a patron of Beverley Races, but for more refined tastes there were the Assembly Rooms (for dancing and cards), a theatre, a circulating library and concerts. The correspondence and later writings of Mary Wollstonecraft give us tantalising glimpses of the culture of this vanished age and reveal something of the privileged, if tedious, existence of being a young lady at that time. For most well-to-do parents their daughter's future lay in making a good marriage, rearing children and running a household – not in pursuing a career or paid employment. For girls an education was often seen as a way of making them marriageable and ladylike. Yet, in the important business of finding a suitable husband for their daughter the Wollstonecrafts probably realised that they had a difficult task on their hands for Mary was 'sharp in manner and often angry in appearance'.

For a lively, intelligent and emotional girl like Mary Wollstonecraft the restrictions on her freedom of action must have been irksome in the extreme. Although she was to later to describe her Beverley years as ones of 'serenity', it seems clear her family life was less than ideal. Her memoirs point to a father who was both feckless and violent and to an over-strict mother who favoured Mary's older brother, Ned.

Edward Wollstonecraft seems to have been a highly unpleasant individual who, to compensate for his failings, spent much of his time squandering his inheritance, drinking and abusing his family. As well as having to endure her father's violence herself Mary records that she was sometimes forced to sleep on the landing to protect her mother from his drunken rages. Goaded by her experiences of a dysfunctional family and what she perceived as a lack of parental love Mary was later to write: 'I never had a father'. Her childhood experiences seem to have had a profound effect on her and on her opinions about marriage for she was to declare that she would never marry 'for interested motives or endure a life of dependence'.

Seemingly unloved by both her father and her mother Mary sought solace from friendships and in particular from her relationship with fellow-Beverlonian Jane Arden. Jane was a girl of similar age, with whom she developed an intense and demanding friendship as shown in a series of letters beginning in 1773.

In spite of Edward Wollstonecraft's apparent scorn for the notion of female education Mary had experienced enough schooling to discover that she had a talent for writing although she was deeply

Mary Wollstonecraft and Jane Arden enjoyed long walks together on Beverley's historic Westwood Pastures.

aware of her educational shortcomings (for example, her poor standard of French) in comparison to her friend. This is hardly surprising since Jane was the daughter of itinerant lecturer, John Arden, who gave public lectures on science and literary subjects and proudly described himself as a 'philosopher'. Arden worked as an agent for the great Catholic landowner, William Constable, one of the East Riding's foremost patrons in the late eighteenth century.

Mary Wollstonecraft probably first met Jane Arden at one of John Arden's lectures and she firmly attached herself to the Arden household in order to nurture her friendship with Jane and benefit from the kind of education that John Arden's children were receiving. As Jane was to discover, Mary's friendship could be extremely demanding; Mary's ego would not countenance any rival, nor was she prepared to be taken for granted by her new friend. Full of self-importance at times (and self-pity at others) and with a volatile, attention-seeking nature, Mary's literary rebukes could be devastating. After a 'falling-out' in late 1774, for example, she was to write: 'your behaviour hurt me extremely and your not answering my letter shows that you set little value on my friendship.'

Mary Wollstonecraft's relationships with other girls, who she saw as rivals for Jane's attention, could be equally quarrelsome and of one of Jane's friends she was to write: 'for my part all animosities have ceased'.

Yet the quarrel with Jane Arden was eventually healed despite Mary's insufferable arrogance when she wrote: 'I must have the first place or none.'

For polite society regular church attendance at Beverley's minster church (or at St Mary's) was expected. We know that Mary Wollstonecraft and Jane Arden went there together.

An American portrait of Mary Wollstonecraft from 1804 based on a picture by John Opie.

The evidence of Mary's letters to Jane Arden also help to give Beverley life of the time a more human face. Taking exercise on Beverley's extensive common lands was then, as now, an acknowledged pleasure and in one of Mary's letters she said: 'I long for a walk in my darling Westwood.'

There are other references to theatregoing, for Beverley was on the circuit of York theatre companies who played at a purpose-built playhouse in Walkergate. In a letter of late May 1773 Mary wrote: 'I intend going to see *The Macaroni* if it be performed and expect a great deal of pleasure.'

Of course, for polite society churchgoing was, in the late eighteenth century, part of the fabric of life both for religious and social reasons. A short walk along Highgate from the Wollstonecraft's house in Wednesday Market stood Beverley's imposing minster church and on Sundays we know that both Mary and Jane attended together. However, during their quarrel Mary was to write in aggrieved tones: 'you have insinuated that I dared to profane so sacred a place with idle chit-chat.'

The Beverley period of Mary Wollstonecraft's life came to a sudden end when her father decided to quit the town and return to London (1775). She had lived in the Beverley area from the age of nine to the age of fifteen (longer than she would live anywhere else) and she retained fond memories of the place and of her girlhood friendship with Jane Arden for many years to come. However, twenty years later after a hard life spent as a lady's companion, teacher and above all as a writer she was able to make a return visit to the town (June 1795). Aged thirty-six and having travelled extensively in Ireland, France and Scandinavia she was now less impressed with Beverley but was as outspoken as ever:

> The town did not please me quite so well as formerly – it appeared so diminutive; and when I found that many of the inhabitants had lived in the same houses ever since I left it, I would not help wondering how they could thus have vegetated.

In fact she might have been referring to Jane Arden since her childhood friend was still living there and had been running a successful school since 1784. The brief visit of 1795 was in fact her final look at Beverley, for two years later she was dead from blood poisoning following complications after the birth of her second daughter.

In many ways the life of Mary Wollstonecraft was a tragic one and her early death at the age of thirty-eight might confirm that view. However, as England's first feminist she gained an ultimate immortality among succeeding generations of women struggling to win both political rights and equality of opportunity in the two centuries after her death.

6

Navigating the Riding

In the twenty-first century the road haulage industry dominates the movement of freight with trucks carrying more than 98 per cent of the goods purchased in Britain. This is hardly surprising since lorries offer significant advantages in the point-to-point delivery of goods to customers. The rise of Britain's road haulage industry in the last hundred years has, however, taken place at the expense of the railways. In the same way, the faster movement of goods by train in the nineteenth century helped to undermine the transport of foodstuffs, raw materials and finished products by river and canal…

In the sparsely populated rural East Yorkshire of yesteryear, dominated by the needs of farming, natural rivers were important for the movement of merchandise especially when road transport by horse-drawn wagon was both difficult and expensive. The River Hull had long been used for the transport of bulky materials and in the twelfth century, for example, the abbey at Meaux (north of Wawne) was constructed from stone brought by river from quarries in the Brough/Brantingham area.

In the same way the developing town of Beverley was able to make use of the natural tideway of the River Hull for its growing trade in wool. Since the river was about one mile away from the town the merchants of medieval Beverley made use of a beck or creek flowing into it and fed by watercourses that once ran through the town's main streets. By the end of the twelfth century a canalised Beverley Beck, three-quarters of a mile long and with its banks shored up with brick and timber, seems to have become the water-borne entrance to the town. This was five centuries before the Industrial Revolution and the 'age' of canals!

Sea-going vessels loaded with raw wool established prosperous trading links with Flemish merchants in the cloth towns of the Low Countries (like Ypres and Damme). The present-day area of Beckside (the limit of navigation) must then have been a lively and bustling place for in the thirteenth century Beverley men were among some of Yorkshire's greatest exporters of raw wool. The town was also able to build up its own cloth industry supplied by wool from the extensive flocks of East Yorkshire (like those of Meaux Abbey which in 1280 had 11,000 sheep). Beverley's links with the medieval trade in raw wool and with the manufacture of woollen cloth live on to this day through street names like Flemingate (originally called Flammengaria after the Flemish merchants who traded there) and Dyer Lane (named after those who dyed cloth like the internationally famous Beverley Scarlets of the late thirteenth century).

For centuries Beverley Beck continued to be a major commercial artery for the town and the area around it remained at the heart of industries like leather tanning. The maintenance of the beck and of keeping the River Hull downstream to the Humber clear of obstructions was of major concern to Beverley Corporation for beck tolls were a major source of their income. Under an Act passed in 1726 during the reign of George I, for example, the Corporation was empowered to cleanse, deepen and widen this ancient tidal waterway while at the beginning of the nineteenth century the building of lock gates at its junction with the River Hull made it possible to maintain the level of the water constant at all times.

The Canal head at Pocklington. The Pocklington Canal was promoted by an Act of Parliament in 1815 and took three years to build. Coal, lime fertiliser and industrial goods were carried to Pocklington and farm produce was sent via the canal and the River Derwent to the West Riding.

Upstream from Beverley navigation of the River Hull was more difficult, although by the seventeenth century there was a regular water-borne trade as far as Wansford. Through the opening of the Bridgewater Canal in 1761 engineers like James Brindley had begun to show the possibilities of developing water-borne transport for commodities like coal. Following the example set by Brindley and others enterprising individuals at Driffield (led by William Porter, the innkeeper of the Blue Bell) were quick to realise the opportunities of improving the upper reaches of the River Hull for the benefit of trade and by December 1766 the Lincolnshire engineer John Grundy had produced a report for an improved navigation. Under an Act of Parliament passed in the following year local commissioners were given the power to improve the River Hull from its junction with Aike Beck to Fisholme and to build a five-mile-long canal to join it to Driffield itself. The work, including four locks built to accommodate 'Driffield-sized keels', cost £13,000 and was complete by May 1770. A toll collector was appointed at a salary of £40 a year and realistic charges of 3s a ton set for general merchandise. Yet trade did not develop as rapidly as had been hoped partly because of problems at Hull Bridge (Tickton) outside the jurisdiction of the commissioners and because of silting-up of the river. Yet despite these issues warehouses were soon being built at the Driffield canal basin and a further Act of Parliament passed in 1801 enabled the commissioners to deal with their earlier difficulties. By the 1830s the Driffield Navigation was more prosperous and was being used to bring in coal from the West Riding, timber from Hull and to 'export' wool, corn and other farm produce from the Driffield area.

The enthusiasm in the East Riding for improved waterway links were soon to set in motion even more ambitious schemes by landowners around Market Weighton. Five years after Parliament had approved the Driffield Navigation, a nine-and-a-half-mile-long canal to link the town with the Humber Estuary gained parliamentary approval. Around £12,000 was raised to build the canal from about thirty-seven subscribers but they had to wait a considerable time to see a return on their investment.

The beginnings of the Market Weighton Canal Project were marked by indecision and controversy with a bewildering number of changes of key personnel. At first the commissioners seemed to favour John Grundy as their choice of engineer but his plans were then rejected as too costly. By the time of their first formal meeting (held at the Black Swan in Market Weighton on 12 June 1772) the canal plans of the Yorkshire engineer John Smith seemed to be in favour but by the end of August these too had been rejected (on Grundy's advice) and Grundy himself was back in charge. In the event the whole scheme was dogged by financial crises and delays and it was not until ten years later (in 1782) that the canal was finally completed. Even then financial necessity meant that the canal stopped two miles southwest of Market Weighton itself.

Yet, despite the problems of the Market Weighton Canal this did not discourage others from launching their own less ambitious schemes. Perhaps seeking to profit from the enthusiasm for new waterways (marked by the 'canal mania' of the 1790s) rich local landowners hatched their own plans. Around the village of Lockington the Hotham family held sway and around 1798 they made the stream called Aike Beck navigable by providing locks, a short artificial cut and a landing place/coal wharf about two miles east of the village. Similarly, close to the village of Leven, east of Beverley, the Bethell Family of Rise Hall owned extensive estates. In 1799 the newly widowed Charlotte Bethell asked the experienced canal engineer, William Jessop, to undertake a survey for a three-mile-long canal to link the village of Leven with the River Hull. In March 1800 he estimated that a canal could be built for £4,041 and the following year Charlotte, at her own expense, secured an Act of Parliament to allow the work to commence. In an age of business dominated by men the enterprise of Charlotte Bethell in promoting her own canal must be unique!

It seems that the Leven Canal cost more than intended for in 1805 Charlotte Bethell obtained a second Act of Parliament allowing her to increase the tolls she could charge on shipments of coal, corn, lime and other merchandise. Despite these 'teething troubles' the canal remained in commercial use until 1935 surviving the coming of the railway to the area in 1864 (the Hull to Hornsea line).

A poster advising of repairs to the Market Weighton Canal in 1868 during Cave Fair Week.

Of all the important communities in the East Riding in the late eighteenth and early nineteenth centuries it was Pocklington that had to wait longest for a canal link. A waterway from the River Derwent to the town had first been mooted in 1777 but it was not until 1801 that a public meeting was held to discuss the idea and it took a further fourteen years before an Act of Parliament was secured! George Leather Junior had surveyed the route selected between 1813 and 1814 and the young engineer had estimated the cost of an eight-mile-long canal (with eight locks) at £43,630 or £51,887 if the canal was taken completely into Pocklington itself. In the event the cheaper option was chosen and the canal opened three years later for a sum less than the estimate! In the early years at least attempts were made to develop a canal trade at Pocklington and a directory of 1823 declared that: 'the Union Packet sails alternately from Pocklington Canal Head to Tummon and Smithson's wharf, High Street, Hull, and from thence to Pocklington Canal Head every week.'

As usual with undertakings of this kind the principal shareholders were titled landowners like Earl Fitzwilliam who invested £3,000 and Lord Muncaster who invested £1,000. However, there were also smaller shareholders, for example, local tradesmen and Pocklington townsfolk who clearly believed that the new canal had a promising future. They were soon to be disappointed for the Pocklington Canal largely served an agricultural district and although some dividends were paid after 1830 the return on their investments was poor.

Further problems were soon apparent for after only thirty years of its working life the canal faced a more efficient rival: the railway. By August 1845 there were plans for a new line linking York, Pocklington and Market Weighton and it was soon recognised that the canal would lose out to a form

Beverley Beck in the 1930s. Despite competition from the railways there was still a healthy traffic in keelboats using the beck until the Second World War. This was the industrial area of Beverley and the beck served Hodgson's Tannery and the animal feedstuff business of Barker & Lee Smith Ltd (their wharf is on the left of the image).

of transport that was both faster and cheaper. When the line opened in October 1847 the shareholders of the Pocklington Canal quickly came to terms with the York & North Midland Railway and sold out to their rival (November 1847). It was a similar story with the Market Weighton Canal where the canal subscribers were bought out by the railway in 1850 for the sum of £14,405. Thereafter the traffic carried by both canals saw a steady decline until by 1900 it was in a moribund state.

Although the coming of railways to East Yorkshire posed a challenge to transportation by river and canal the competition was not always immediately fatal. The Driffield Navigation remained independent of the railways and by cutting tolls was able to compete with the Hull to Bridlington Railway (1846) and even forestall the opening of new railway branches. Yet, although there were some new opportunities for traffic, like linseed cake and artificial fertilisers, there was also a steady decline in other areas like coal and grain. The decline was even more marked after the development of the road-haulage industry in the 1920s and 1930s. The last commercial vessel to unload its cargo of wheat at Driffield was the keel *Caroline* in March 1945.

With commercial traffic now gone East Yorkshire's system of rivers and canals is but a shadow of its former self and more concerned, these days, with leisure pursuits than trade and industry. Yet, much has been done in recent times to preserve the heritage aspects of the area's waterways. At Beverley new housing has replaced derelict industrial buildings alongside the Beck and thereby created a very desirable place to live. Meanwhile at Driffield and Pocklington enthusiasts are keen to overturn the ravages of time and restore both navigations to their former glory for the benefit of future generations.

The head of Beverley Beck in October 2007 showing the dramatic changes of recent years. Gone are the mills and industrial buildings of the 1930s to be replaced by waterside housing.

7

The 'Third Man' in Hull Elections

In the twenty-first century Members of Parliament expect to be well paid for their duties as representatives of the people and these days earn in excess of £60,000 a year (plus other expenses). In fact the 'modern-day' payment of MPs only began in 1911 when they received £400 a year. Before this it was expected that they would support themselves and this usually meant that that only those of 'independent means' could stand. In Hull's parliamentary elections of the late eighteenth and early nineteenth the candidates were often local gentry or merchants (or were outsiders supported by wealthy local patrons) and in disputed contests they could expect to pay heavily to win the support of a corrupt electorate…

In a democratic age dominated by party politics it is difficult to imagine a time when election results were determined, not by policies, but by the manipulation and bribery of a small electorate. The growing port of Hull had been sending two representatives to Parliament since 1304, but the right to vote belonged only to the freemen of the town (whether they lived in Hull or not).

The candidates were generally drawn from the upper echelons of society and could sometimes rely on the support of wealthy local patrons like the Maisters, the Sykes, and the Savilles. It was the influence of Sir George Saville, for example, that allowed an outsider, David Hartley of Putney in Surrey, to stand and triumph in the Hull election of 1774. Six years later however Hartley came third in a three-way contest involving William Wilberforce and Lord Robert Manners.

As the eighteenth century progressed Hull's freemen became increasingly concerned that there should be a 'third man' at election time so that there would be a contest in which the candidates would have to spend money in bribes and in 'treats'. Between 1701 and 1767 there were twenty parliamentary elections in Hull but only five of these were contested, whereas between 1768 and 1830 there were seventeen elections in which twelve were contested. The notebook of Robert Broadley held in the Hull University Archive is particularly revealing about the cost of such disputed elections, for it gives details of the 1768 election between William Weddell, Lord Robert Manners and Captain Thomas Lee. According to Broadley about 850 freemen had cast their votes before Captain Lee withdrew from the contest (having already spent about £3,000). He also revealed that both William Weddell and Thomas Manners both gave each of their voters two guineas per man and that the election cost them £5,000 and £8,000 respectively. These were huge sums by eighteenth-century standards and reflect not only the wholesale bribery of the electors but also the many incidental expenses that had to be borne by the candidates (like the two guineas in expenses paid to the Sheriff of Hull who acted as returning officer). More dubious was the hiring of 'messengers' for, as one observer of Hull elections claimed, upwards of 300 of these assistants or runners were engaged to do nothing at 5s a day merely because they threatened otherwise to go to one of the other candidates!

Another source of expense to the candidates was the arrival of 'out-voters': non-resident freemen who expected to be 'compensated' for the distances they travelled and for their 'living expenses' while they were present in the town. Innkeepers played an important part in the elections of the period and freemen (resident and non-resident) were issued with tickets that enabled them to obtain

Portrait of David Hartley, elected MP for Hull in 1774–1780.

food and drink. Broadley estimated, in 1768, that there were about seventy Hull Freemen resident in London, of whom 'about ten or twelve came down.'

The contempt of Hull's wealthier citizens (and of the press in the reporting of elections) towards these corrupt non-resident freemen was a feature of the times. In 1778 Hull's first dock had been opened and the success of this meant that the Corporation and the merchant interest wanted MPs who would promote new initiatives for the port's growth. A 'third man' was often of little use to them and if a contested election led to the premature retirement or defeat of a sitting MP these leading citizens sometimes gave vent to their feelings. Samuel Thornton, one of Hull's representatives from 1784, had given his assistance in promoting a bill to make additional dock room in Hull. In 1806 however Thornton was defeated and the mayor and Corporation sent him a letter of regret and showed their disapproval of 'a fickle and misguided populace.'

More regrets were expressed during the 1818 election. In June of that year the mayor of Hull gave a speech in which he lamented the decision of one of Hull's long-serving MPs, John Staniforth, not to stand again. Staniforth had first been elected in 1802 and despite his work on behalf of the town the mayor claimed that there were those:

who did not want a man to act but a man to pay: large numbers of out-voters, unconnected with the town by residence and little interested in its prosperity have made demands of the most absurd and extravagant description.

In the event Staniforth decided take part in the 1818 election and although all the employees of the Corporation voted for him he came third. His defeat was lamented too by the *Hull Advertiser* newspaper when it said: 'we think Mr Staniforth has been ill-used.'

Any appeal for greater purity at election time usually fell on deaf ears and this was shown by the campaign of William Bell, a local bookseller and a 'third man' in the election of 1802. Bell's campaign

In 1778 Hull's first dock had been opened and the success of this meant that the Corporation and the merchant interest wanted MPs who would promote new initiatives for the port's growth.

was based on a tirade against bribery and corruption, calling it: 'the keystone of infamy, the defeat of liberty, the germ of slavery and the assassin of the constitution.' However, his campaign was a failure among Hull's freemen, by now used to exploiting the generosity of candidates, and Bell only received three votes! By the beginning of the nineteenth century the clamour for a 'third man' was such that in 1818: 'A great number of the lower order stopped a gentleman who was passing through the town, who was a perfect stranger to them, and offered to support him if he would become their champion.'

The gentleman in question was George Denys who at the time was on his way to contest one of the nearby seats at Beverley. However, these actions do suggest a greedy electorate for, as Hull's *Rockingham* newspaper suggested, the irresistible claims of a 'third man' rested on his ability to pay the customary bribes and would have: 'brought into Parliament a chimney sweeper or a walking broomstick possessed of the will and the way to make the usual compliment to his friends.'

Defaulting on 'polling money' was often seen as an unpardonable sin. In 1826 it was said that one of the sitting members, John Mitchell, dared not appear before his constituents because he had not paid polling money from the last election!

Bribery of electors, although illegal, took place at Hull and elsewhere because of the difficulty (and expense) of proving that it had taken place. The House of Commons was petitioned about the result of elections in Hull on five occasions between 1700 and 1832, but these petitions were either withdrawn or not proceeded with. The task of proving that bribery had taken place was difficult for the money was made to pass from the candidate's account to the pockets of the freemen by circuitous and often untraceable routes. Without a proper scrutiny of election expenses (which did not come until the Corrupt Practices Act of the late nineteenth century) policing the conduct of the candidates was almost impossible.

Sharp practice at election times in Hull was not restricted to just bribery and treating. The way people had voted could be seen in the polling books published after the election and so intimidation could be brought to bear on vulnerable freemen through the threat of dismissal from employment,

The artist William Hogarth depicted scenes from an election in Oxfordshire in 1754 but the same kinds of election malpractice also took place in Hull. The picture is entitled *Canvassing for Votes*. In the foreground of the picture two election agents both try to bribe the same voter.

termination of a tenancy or by a refusal to continue patronage. At Hull in 1724, for example, it was said that Thomas Proctor, anchor smith, was turned out of a position worth £20 per year because he voted for the 'wrong' candidate. Other examples of malpractice emerged during the scrutiny that took place after the 1818 election. This had produced a close result with only thirty-eight votes separating the second and third place candidates (James Graham and John Staniforth). The scrutiny revealed the scope for 'identity fraud' at a time when birth or death certificates did not exist. At the hearing a Jacob Beharril was questioned; Beharil had, during the poll, impersonated John Dickinson, late of Gainsborough in Lincolnshire, who had been dead for some years. The *Hull Advertiser* of 18 July 1818 recorded in stark detail the circumstances of this fraud:

> He stated in the court that some of the Orange Party (Graham) had asked him if he was free of Hull and on his answering 'no', the same gentleman asked him if he knew the above John Dickinson. On his answering 'yes', they invited him to vote for Mr Graham which he did.

Similar trickery was uncovered when it was revealed that the votes of three seamen had been 'cast' when they were away at sea on voyages to Antwerp or Greenland! In the event the scrutiny made no difference to the final result; James Graham was still elected, but by the narrower margin of just four votes!

Seats in Parliament could be fiercely contested. The wealth of William Wilberforce (derived from trade) meant that he was able to stand for election as MP for Hull. The election of 1780 is said to have cost him £8,000. (Murray Close © 2006 Bristol Bay Productions LLC; Ioan Grufford as William Wilberforce in the House of Commons [from *Amazing Grace*, a Samuel Goldwyn/Roadside Attractions Film])

At a time of inadequate policing the events of 1818 also revealed the violence that often took place at election time, especially when polling took place over two or three days. The *Hull Advertiser* of 20 June 1818 reported the warnings of the Lord Mayor to the crowds at the hustings that:

> *Various acts of violence had been committed the previous day, that several additional constables had been appointed and that those guilty of violence would be brought to justice whatever party they belonged to.*

In fact some candidates seemed to prepare themselves for such violence. At the 1780 election, for instance, William Wilberforce was taken by his election agents to visit a stalwart butcher; somewhat shrinking from shaking hands with him he said to one of his friends that he thought it going rather too low for votes. 'Oh Sir,' was the reply, 'he is a fine fellow if you come to bruising!'

It would however be easy to overestimate the part that elections played in the violence of the times. In an age before the establishment of regular police forces disorder was common; the excitement of election time together with copious amounts of free alcohol provided at the expense of candidates merely provided the opportunity to settle scores. In this respect Hull was really no better or worse than many other towns in England. Yet the venality of the Hull electorate (and other towns), together with a growing middle-class morality, was ultimately to bring in reforms that put an end to the worst features of the old system.

8

The Winds of Change at Skidby

One of the most controversial political issues of recent times has been that of wind farms with supporters and opponents locked into a propaganda war about their merits and drawbacks. East Yorkshire's first wind farm of seven turbines was opened at Out Newton near Easington in 2002 and a further one of twelve turbines was approved for Lissett Airfield, near Hornsea in February 2007. However wind power has been used for centuries in the form of windmills and in the nineteenth century there were over 200 of them in the East Riding alone. Yet only one operational mill now remains: the famous Skidby Mill, built in 1821…

Of all the romantic images conjured up by a rural countryside of yesteryear perhaps none is more seductive than that of the old windmill with its creaking sails turning slowly in the breeze. For those who regularly travel on the A164 road between Beverley and the Humber Bridge the towering presence of Skidby Mill is a constant reminder of this vanished world.

The village of Skidby probably dates back to Anglo-Saxon times and the name is thought to mean 'dirty farm'. The village was built on the sides of a dry valley with its single main street bending awkwardly around rising ground occupied by the church of St Michael. The land for the church was given by Walter de Gray in the year 1227, but the variety of stone, rubble and brick used to build it suggests that it was constructed over a period of time perhaps from any materials that were available to hand. The Revd Arthur Hill, writing about the history of St Michael's in 1976, hinted at his disappointment with the fabric of the church when he wrote that it was: 'mean and humble in appearance.'

This, however, is not a view shared by other Skidby dwellers. Mrs Marion Mooney moved to Skidby eight years ago and she described the church as 'simple and beautiful' while her husband Nick suggested that St Michael's was a church best appreciated from the inside.

Like all East Riding villages of the past the main occupation until recent times was farming and a directory of 1823 lists eight of them with other supporting trades like a blacksmith, a carpenter and a miller. In 1823 the miller was William Watson but the craft he represented in the village was much older for there had been a windmill at Skidby since the fourteenth century.

Today's windmill at Skidby had in fact been built for William Watson in 1821 by Hull millwrights Norman & Smithson, but originally it had been a much smaller structure. In 1854 Joseph Thompson purchased the windmill and it was he who altered it to its present height of five stories. The survival of Skidby Mill, when others in the East Riding went out of business and fell into disrepair, owed much to the Thompson family. In the late nineteenth century the growing international trade in grain meant a large-scale importation of Canadian wheat that was too 'hard' to grind using traditional millstones. Steam-driven roller mills were established in ports like Hull to grind wheat into flour. The Thompson's owned such a mill in Hull but kept Skidby Mill in business to grind barley and oats for animal feed.

The Thompson family were, in fact, vital in ensuring the survival of the windmill for they kept it in good working order until the 1950s and later encouraged its sale to Beverley Rural District Council for the nominal sum of £1 to ensure its preservation.

The church of St Michael with its combination of stone and brick clearly visible.

These days the windmill is owned by the East Riding County Council and forms the centrepiece of the Museum of East Riding Rural Life, one of the area's most important tourist attractions. Since November 2006 David Andrews has been the miller at Skidby. David was formerly the postmaster of the village of Burton Pidsea, east of Hull, but at the age of thirty-seven he saw the job of miller advertised in the *Hull Daily Mail* and recognised it as a golden opportunity for a mid-life career change! In the months since his appointment David has been trained in the art of milling by Skidby resident Peter Willoughby (a volunteer at the windmill for the last seventeen years).

David paid tribute to the importance of voluntary effort in running the operation: 'Skidby Mill is now open every day from 10 a.m. to 5 p.m. and the five volunteers we have are vital in ensuring our success.'

One of these volunteers, Glenda Charlesworth, can often be seen weighing bags of wholemeal flour made from wheat grown in Skidby and ground at the mill. Glenda is studying for an archaeology degree at Hull University and works as a volunteer for two days a week. As she enthused: 'Windmills have been in my blood ever since I worked at Green's Windmill near Nottingham and I find my work as a volunteer here very rewarding.'

Just as the windmill represents the ancient face of Skidby, the building standing in its shadow represents a modern aspect of the village. The Millhouse Restaurant at Skidby is familiar to many people in the East Riding and is famous throughout the region for its award-winning cuisine. A millstone near the entrance to its car park gives a clue to the origins of the place for an attached plaque says: 'Welcome to Franco's Restaurant.' Franco Ciuffetelli emigrated to England from the Abruzzo region of Italy in the 1960s and eventually settled in Hull. His success with Franco's Restaurant in Cottingham led to him buying the

Skidby Mill: the only working windmill east of the Pennines. The present mill dates from 1821, but was altered to its present five storeys by Joseph Thompson after 1854. The brick tower is painted with black bitumen to prevent damp penetration. The fantail at the back of the white cap moves the sails into the wind.

White Lodge in Skidby and converting it into the Millhouse Restaurant (opened 1990). Although, sadly, Franco Ciuffetelli died in 1994, his son Marc took over and under his guidance the restaurant has gone from strength to strength. The general manager is Mrzic Dusko (from the former Yugoslavia) and he has worked for the Ciuffetelli family since 1989. He explained the success of the business in these terms: 'We employ thirty full-time and part-time staff including ten chefs and the quality ingredients we use in the restaurant are sourced locally. During our busiest time in December we prepare over 200 meals a day.'

An even older example of Skidby's hospitality industry is the Half Moon Inn on the main street. These days it is both a public house and a restaurant famous for its giant Yorkshire puddings, but it has been operating in the village since at least 1823. Village publicans in former times often carried out occupations other than serving thirsty customers and from a directory of 1892 we learn that the landlord, William Harrison, was also a market gardener.

This same directory also shows the importance of the agrarian economy in the village of the time for it lists seven farmers and eleven market gardeners. Travelling along Skidby's main street you can get a flavour of this agricultural past since some substantial farmhouses from the eighteenth and nineteenth centuries remain.

Until recently a post office was often regarded as an important community asset. A local directory of 1857, for example, records that Christopher Hutchinson was Skidby's postmaster, but he also made and repaired boots and shoes too! By 1892 George Cargill, the parish clerk, was running the post office combined with a grocery and drapery business. A directory of that year recorded the arrival of mail at 8.10 a.m. and the dispatch of letters from Skidby at 5.00 p.m. More than a century later the village post offie was being run from a portakabin next to the Methodist church, but in October 2007 it was earmarked for closure in a new round of cuts to the rural post-office network.

One aspect of Skidby's friendly community appeal today is the village hall built in 1928 on land provided by the Thompson family and these days home to a number of activities including art, embroidery, bridge and yoga.

Change and continuity are facets of any community and Skidby is no exception. A hundred years ago the village had two shopkeepers, two tailors, two shoemakers and a blacksmith supported in 1901 by a population of just 356 people. Yet by 2001 these occupations had all but disappeared even though the population had grown to 1,356. However, as Helen Kool, who works part-time in the village for her brother's engineering business (J. Kool Engineers), pointed out: 'the disappearance of Skidby's shopkeepers owes much to the proximity of the shops and supermarkets of nearby Cottingham and Beverley which are these days more accessible by car.'

Yet as some trades disappeared other businesses have taken their place. A good example is the firm of JMJ Woodworking Machinery Ltd owned by John Jenkinson and occupying the former site of the village garage and filling station. The company employs ten people and moved here from Beverley over twenty years ago. Helped by its location and good road access the firm sells industrial woodworking machinery to customers all over Yorkshire.

Through its historic windmill, a welcoming public house dating back to the nineteenth century and, at its heart, an ancient village church Skidby has preserved its links with the past. However, with vibrant modern businesses like the acclaimed Millhouse Restaurant, JMJ Woodworking Machinery Ltd and JKE it is also a community for the present and the future.

9

When Cholera Came Calling

One of the features of life in the twenty-first century is the media spotlight on health scares with hospital 'superbugs' and the threat of 'avian flu' just two of the issues highlighted in sensationalist news reporting. Yet in dealing with present-day threats to our health medical science has never been in a stronger position to provide the answers needed. These days, well-equipped research laboratories are vigilant in seeking out the causes of illness while a multi-million pound drug industry is eager to supply the remedies. Two hundred years ago the East Riding, along with other parts of the UK, was in a far less favourable position to meet the challenge of epidemics caused by poor standards of public health and a woeful ignorance of the causes of disease. Nowhere was this more apparent than in responses to a deadly new invader from the east: Asiatic cholera…

A major feature of the early nineteenth century was the rapid growth of towns and cities and this trend was as apparent in the East Riding as it was elsewhere in Britain. Between 1831 and 1861, for example, Hull grew from a town of 12,000 houses to one of 20,000 due to both a natural increase in the population and by attracting newcomers (for example, the Irish) arriving in search of employment. Many of the features of modern life that today we take for granted (like planning controls, decent sanitation, refuse collection and a pure water supply) were absent from a place that expanded outwards from the old town along Hessle Road and Beverley Road. Like in most growing industrial cities of the time the housing needs of this growing population led to the creation of narrow courts and alleys of damp, ill-ventilated houses built back-to-back (often shared by several families) with outside privies and a communal pump or tap for their water supply.

It is against this background of overcrowded, unsanitary slums that the devastating arrival of Asiatic cholera must be seen. In 1831 *Cholera Morbus*, a water-borne disease endemic in India, was virtually unknown in Britain. However, travelling along trade routes this deadly disease had reached Europe by 1826 and, via ships trading with Germany, reached Sunderland in October 1831. Within months the disease was reported at Goole with Hull under attack soon after. According to the *Hull Advertiser* of 20 April 1832 the worst-affected districts were the narrow courts and alleys of the Witham/Wincolmlee area and in the six months that followed there were 270 deaths from cholera.

Apart from the laissez-faire attitudes of the time, part of the problem in dealing with cholera was that medical opinion had no clear idea on the cause of the disease. It was only with Louis Pasteur's experiments in the 1860s that the germ theory of disease came about and it was not until 1885 that the German scientist Robert Koch discovered the specific bacteria that caused cholera. The truth was that the disease was spread when water supplies became polluted by the excrement of cholera victims, but until this became known doctors continued to believe that cholera was simply associated with filth or some poisonous miasma in the air. Campaigners like Edward Collins, editor of the *Hull Advertiser*, launched numerous attacks on the complacent sanitary authorities in Hull for their failure to take action on issues like inadequate sewerage, filthy streets, stinking dunghills and the like but the real culprit was an inadequate water supply drawn from underground sources polluted by the sewage of nearby privies or, after 1845, from the River Hull at the new waterworks built by Hull Corporation at Stoneferry.

Drawing from *The Lancet* of an early cholera victim in Sunderland.

This was the same river water that had been polluted by effluent entering it from the drains of Driffield and Beverley! At an early stage there were complaints about the quality of the water from the new Stoneferry works even though it had been filtered. Those Hull folk who could afford it sometimes chose to buy their water at 1d a bucket supplied by watermen from springs west of Hull, and this action probably saved their lives, for in the summer of 1849 a new outbreak of cholera, far worse than that of 1832, began. On 3 August the *Hull Advertiser* recorded, 'Great alarm has existed in the Groves during the last two days originated by the death of a female employed at the cotton mills after an attack by cholera.'

By the end of August the newspaper was reporting deaths on a weekly basis and the issue of 7 September reported a death toll of 379 in total. In this edition Collins, championing the cause of poor and most vulnerable, launched a scathing attack on the 'so-called Sanitary Committee' pointing out that cholera was not a divine visitation and that those who died of it were 'victims of human neglect, ignorance and social wrong.'

James Sibree, chaplain of the Hull General Cemetery Co., confirmed the opinions of Edward Collins when he wrote: 'There was much apathy on the part of the authorities of the town as to sanitary arrangements.'

Sibree was to write perhaps some of the most harrowing accounts of the 1849 cholera epidemic for he was present at a vast number of interments at the cemetery on Spring Bank during August and September. He recorded that the men employed in digging graves worked both by day and by night and recalled 9 September as a particularly awful day when he witnessed funeral processions occupying the entire space between Beverley Road and the cemetery gates. He said: 'I cannot think of it without terror – I interred forty-three bodies of my fellow citizens.'

Sibree's labours also included visiting those who were sick or dying and he spent one afternoon among the cottages of New Village and Vauxhall Gardens on Hessle Road. He recalled: 'In the first poor dwelling on the ground lay a man in the last stage of the disease. His flesh, which I ventured to touch, was awfully discoloured.'

In a dwelling close by he found a woman in agony with stomach cramp while on a table in the same room was laid: 'a child two years old, with a white cloth thrown over it, who had died of the cholera only a few hours before my arrival.'

Above: 'A Court for King Cholera' was a cartoon from *Punch* 1852. Before it was discovered that cholera was spread by impure drinking water, cholera was simply associated with dirt and overcrowding.

Right: Little Lane off Humber Street in Hull was a typical unsanitary working-class slum.

Ineffective measures taken in Hull and other towns included burning barrels of tar in the streets in a forlorn attempt to 'purify the air'.

Some died alone and were left undiscovered until the stench of decay alerted neighbours to their demise. Sibree recounted the story of an aged widow 'residing in the miserable garret of a large house let off in separate rooms to poor families' somewhere close to Blanket Row in the Old Town. Her neighbours discovered 'her shrivelled body, awfully discoloured, cold, stiff and dead and with her knees doubled up by the agonising cramp.'

The writings of Sibree and accounts in the *Hull Advertiser* also indicate the desperate measures taken by the authorities to halt the spread of a disease whose cause was not properly understood. Since it was believed that cholera had arisen from a poisonous miasma, tar barrels were set alight in the streets in a forlorn belief that this would purify the air while the *Hull Advertiser* of 14 September 1849 tells of the 'watering of the streets with a solution of chloride of lime' in order to cleanse them of infection. There were also those who sought to profit from the alarm by offering 'quack remedies' like those of J.C. Reinhardt, Chemist & Druggist of the Market Place in Hull, who sold bottles of their Anti-Cholera Mix at 1s and 2s 6d.

The memorial to Hull's cholera victims in Spring Bank Cemetery, built after the outbreak of 1849.

Hull's cholera epidemic of 1849 resulted in the highest death rate from the disease in the entire country with the total number of fatalities put at 1,834. At its peak in September 1849, 500 people were dying each week and Hull became a ghost town with people from nearby towns and villages refusing to come near (even on market days) lest they catch the deadly infection. However, the lack of a quarantine meant that Hull's inhabitants were able to 'export' the disease elsewhere. Dr John Snow, famous for his research into cholera in the 1850s, wrote about how the infection came to Pocklington in East Yorkshire:

> A man came from Hull (where cholera was prevailing), by trade a painter, his name and age are unknown. He lodged at the house of Samuel Wride, was attacked on his arrival on the 8th September and died on the 9th. Samuel Wride himself was attacked on the 11th September and died shortly afterwards.

This was the start of a major epidemic in Pocklington for those who visited Wride's house themselves contracted the deadly disease and helped to spread it still further to nearby York.

Other people from Hull (who probably left the town in search of work) carried the infection with them and on 24 August 1849 it was reported that there had been ten deaths among the inmates of the Beverley workhouse in Minster Moorgate. Worse hit still was the small town of Hedon (east of Hull) where an Irish immigrant called Bernard Griffith arrived in early September carrying the infection. He was dead within fourteen hours and by mid-September Hedon was in the grip of a major epidemic with the total number of deaths put at fifty (or one in twenty of the population).

The cholera epidemic of 1849 was not the end of the cholera story in Hull for there were other outbreaks in the period 1865-1866 with the disease arriving with immigrants from Europe en route to America. However, after the 1849 epidemic there was a slow improvement in standards of public health despite the rearguard action of the 'muck interest', as the *Hull Advertiser* called them (landlords who objected to paying the higher local taxes needed to pay for improved sanitation).

Most significant was the abandonment of the River Hull as a source of supply in the 1860s after the discovery that Springhead at Anlaby could provide a sufficient supply of pure spring water if boreholes were sunk through the chalk. Nevertheless the terrors of cholera were slow to fade in the public mind while the monument to the dead in Hull's Spring Bank Cemetery provided a more lasting reminder of the need for improved public health.

10

A Rogues Gallery

In modern times we take it for granted that we can call on the services of a sophisticated, well-equipped police force to investigate crimes and to bring the perpetrators to justice. Since 1974 the Humberside force has been responsible for policing both north and south of the River Humber and their neighbourhood policing teams totalling more than 2,000 officers have a budget in excess of £167,000,000 at their disposal. Two centuries ago the detection and prevention of crime was much more uncertain even though the authorities sought to redress the balance by the use of savage punishments on those who were caught…

It was the passing of the Metropolitan Police Act of 1829 that really began the era of modern policing in Britain. This established the first modern police in London and was the work of the Home Secretary Sir Robert Peel (1788-1850). Other parts of the country (including the East Riding) continued to rely on a centuries-old system of community policing by unpaid parish constables elected or chosen to serve for a year. In towns like Hull and Beverley bellmen or watchmen who patrolled the streets at night supported them. Naturally the job of acting as a constable without pay was highly unpopular and some tried to avoid it often at the risk of falling foul of the law themselves. In 1755, for example, we learn of the indictment at the East Riding Quarter Sessions of George Atkinson of Leven, yeoman, for neglecting his duty as constable.

The process of change really began in 1836 with the establishment of police forces in Hull and Beverley. The Hull Police Force began with forty-four constables supervised by a superintendent and other officers. In Beverley the Corporation established a Watch Committee and appointed twenty-four constables to be on night watch of whom seven had to be on duty at any one time. In the country areas of the East Riding, however, the magistrates continued to rely on the system of parish constables and as members of the landowning classes they resisted calls for change claiming that there was no need for better policing. Yet evidence to a Royal Commission on rural policing in 1836 suggested there was a need; Andrew McManus, the chief officer in Hull, claimed that the county often called on him for help at events like Howden Fair when there was potential for disorder.

Opposition to compulsion meant that new legislation gave JPs discretionary powers to establish rural police forces, but those in the East Riding did nothing, believing that such a force was would be expensive and unnecessary and that the existing system was capable of improvement through the appointment of paid superintending constables.

However, it was clear that reform could not be delayed forever and in 1853 there was a new government enquiry into areas still using the discredited parish-constable system. From 1852 plans were being made to build lock-up houses in places like Patrington, Pocklington, Howden and Leven. The police station in Leven was opened in 1852 consisting of three cells and other facilities manned by an inspector, a sergeant and three constables. Yet as the 1856 County Police Bill made its way through Parliament there were those who were determined to keep the cost of the new East Riding Police Force as low as possible. At a meeting on 14 October 1856 it was suggested that only a force of forty-eight ordinary police constables and twelve mounted or superintending constables would be needed at a cost of £4,200 per year! Charles William Strickland, an opponent of police reform, was then elected as chairman of the police committee and he ensured that the new chief constable would be appointed on the lowest salary possible under Home Office rules (i.e. £250 per year).

They appointed Major Bernard Layard (a military officer from York) as the first chief constable and the new East Riding Police began with the swearing in of forty-eight constables at Beverley (24 January 1857). Part of the House of Correction in Beverley's New Walk became a divisional police station with offices for the chief constable and it later became the headquarters of the East Riding Police Force.

By the 1870s the new force was able to make use of the new science of photography to identify suspects and to assist in the detection of crime. An album of some of those convicted survives in the East Riding Archive in Beverley and these, together with documents from the quarter sessions and newspaper reports of the time, provide a fascinating record of criminal activity of more than a century ago. To a modern-day observer the crimes of those who were caught and sentenced to terms of imprisonment (often with hard labour) might seem trivial (e.g. stealing clothes).

Some of the people in the album of convicted offenders had criminal records stretching back over thirty years. Arthur Webb (alias Lane and Wainwright) had been born around 1850 and had been convicted for the first time in May 1875 at Bradford and West Riding Quarter Sessions for stealing a watch. For this offence he was sentenced to six month's imprisonment but two years later was back in court for stealing potatoes (for which he was sentenced to a month in prison). During the 1880s and 1890s Arthur Webb made frequent court appearances at Leeds, Pontefract, Wakefield and Bradford for a host of petty offences mainly involving the theft of small items but on 14 April 1903 was sentenced to five years penal servitude at Hull Quarter Sessions for stealing six watches in his guise as Arthur Lane. Between 1875 and 1911 he spent over twenty-two years in prison.

On 18 October 1902 a report in the *Beverley Guardian* on the trials held at the East Riding Quarter Sessions four days earlier gave a brief mention to the labourer Henry Robinson (aged twenty-eight) who admitted breaking into the house of John Shepherdson at Norton in order to steal clothing. For this offence he was sentenced to three months with hard labour. In fact Robinson's criminal career had begun at York when he was only ten. On the 3 February 1885 he was convicted of stealing 2s 6d and two 'fancy pies'. For these two offences he was sentenced to six strokes of the birch. Some idea of what juvenile birching involved is shown by a report in the *Pall Mall Gazette* of 1887 on the birching of two other boys for theft:

> *The birch consisted of a number of long thin lashes tied to the end of a stick about two feet long. Each lash had a resemblance more to wire than wood. The officer who held the birch stepped forward to administer the punishment. The boy began the most piteous howling and yelling and red marks appeared almost immediately across his buttocks. The constable took pride in the fact that the culprit would not be able to sit down for quite a time.*

The reaction of Henry Robinson to his birching was not recorded but he was soon in trouble again for absconding from the reformatory where he had been sent.

The same edition of the *Beverley Guardian* in October 1902 coyly reported on a sentence of eighteen months imprisonment on Fred Hope for an 'abominable act at Huggate on 26 August'. The files of the East Riding Quarter Sessions were however much more frank in that they recorded the arrest of Hope for: 'unlawfully attempting, feloniously, wickedly and against the order of nature to carnally know one William Johnson.'

Homosexual acts had been an offence punishable by hanging until 1861 and as late as 1885 new legislation prohibited 'gross indecency' between males.

By far the greatest numbers of images from the late nineteenth and early twentieth centuries are of male prisoners. One of the relatively few females depicted is Sarah Rolfe (alias Conley), a forty-year-old charwoman who was found guilty of theft by a jury on 1 January 1901. She had been arrested on 7 December 1900 (together with an accomplice called Maggie Smith) for stealing £43 4s 6d from Alfred Martin of Filey. Sarah Rolfe was sentenced to six months imprisonment with hard labour.

One of the most remarkable features of the criminal justice system at the beginning of the twentieth century was the tendency of those convicted to reoffend despite the severity of the sentences given

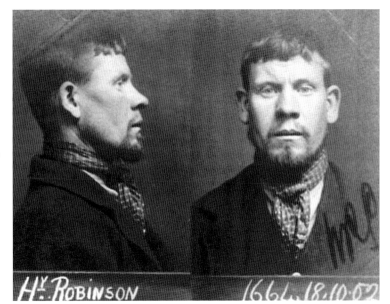

Henry Robinson, taken in October 1902 when he was twenty-eight years old. His criminal career had begun when he was ten. (courtesy of the East Riding Archives Service)

The birching of a juvenile offender in 1887. On 3 February 1885 Henry Robinson had received six strokes of the birch (aged ten) after his appearance at York City Petty Sessions on a charge of stealing half-a-crown and 'two fancy pies'. The birching of juvenile offenders was then commonplace: in 1917 5,210 youths were birched on the orders of magistrates' courts.

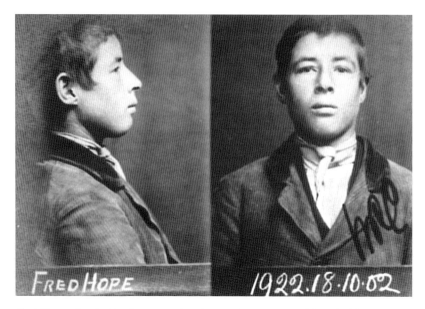

Fred Hope, taken in October 1902 when he was nineteen years old. He had been convicted of committing the 'abominable crime of buggery' at the Yorkshire Wolds village of Huggate on the 26 August 1902. (courtesy of the East Riding Archives Service)

Sarah Rolfe (alias Conley), taken in January 1901 after her conviction for theft at Filey on the 4 December 1900. Her first conviction had been at the Beverley Quarter Sessions on the 8 April 1884 for receiving stolen goods. On this occasion her sentence had been three calendar months with hard labour. She had also appeared nine times before local magistrates between 1874-1900 on lesser charges. (courtesy of the East Riding Archives Service)

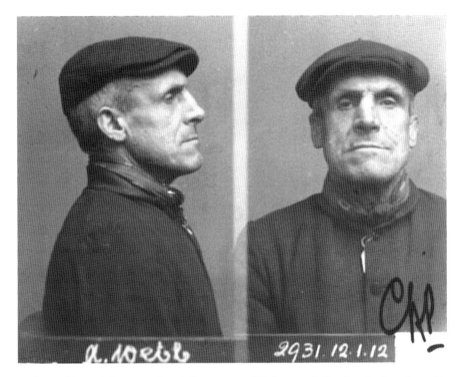

Arthur Webb, aged sixty-two, taken in January 1912. His first conviction dates back to the 10 May 1875 when he was indicted at the Bradford & West Riding Quarter Sessions for stealing a watch under his alias of Matthew Wainwright. (courtesy of the East Riding Archives Service)

to them by the courts. Clearly the punishments often did not have the deterrent effect that the authorities hoped. In the case of the sixty-two-year-old Arthur Webb, for example, he may have become institutionalised by the long periods he spent in prison.

Just like the present day it was particularly horrific crimes that caught the interest of the media. In December 1900, for example, the *News of the World* reported on 'Jack the Ripper type' attacks on women in streets off Hull's Beverley Road. The newspaper said:

> *Within the space of a few hours seven women were stabbed with a knife in the lower part of the abdomen or thigh. In every case after digging the knife into the woman as he passed her the miscreant got clean away.*

Suspicion quickly fell on a hawker and knife grinder called James Gray who had been convicted at Doncaster in 1898 for a similar offence. At an identity parade held at Hull's central police station in Parliament Street he was identified as the man responsible by one of his victims, Edith Hardy, and charged.

Of course, the scale of the problems dealt with by city and town police forces like Hull and Beverley were different to those of the rural East Riding; Beverley continued to have its own separate force until 1928 when it was merged with the East Riding Constabulary. If the writings of Sir Percy Sillitoe (briefly chief constable of the East Riding during 1925) are to be believed: 'the East Riding of Yorkshire was a singularly peaceful and law abiding community with practically no law-breakers at all except for an occasional drunk or poacher.'

Sillitoe had been appointed on a salary of £750 a year (and a house) after a successful career as a policeman in southern Africa and as chief constable of Chesterfield. However, Sillitoe was to fall foul of 'the unwritten code of behaviour' that existed between the local gentry and public servants. On 25 September

1925 one of his constables, PC Parker, patrolling on the North Dalton Road, had become involved in an altercation with Col. Guy Wilson (a local magistrate). According to Sillitoe, Col. Wilson had spoken to the constable in an offensive way and, clearly believing that no one was above the law, he decided to summon Wilson to appear before Pocklington Petty Sessions. Wilson was charged with using abusive language to a police constable and causing a breach of the peace. However, the local aristocracy were clearly incensed that Sillitoe should have taken the word of a humble police constable over that of a titled landowner. With Wilson vehemently denying that he had called the constable a 'damned silly ass' or a 'bloody fool', the Pocklington magistrates dismissed the case.

Perhaps feeling that his own integrity was now in question Sillitoe did not stay in the East Riding much longer and he soon got the job of chief constable of Sheffield on a salary of £1,000 a year. His later career was far more eventful than his time in the East Riding and he earned a formidable reputation as a 'gang-buster' in Sheffield and Glasgow in the 1930s. Between 1946 and 1953 he was the head of MI5 dealing with the problems caused by Soviet spies like Kim Philby, Donald Maclean and Guy Burgess.

As police work became ever more sophisticated forces in the East Riding were able to make use of improved technology to aid their work. Across far-flung country areas maintaining contact between the 'beat-bobby' and his superiors was difficult until the widespread introduction of two-way radios after the Second World War. In the 1920s the only way for a duty sergeant to maintain contact with a patrolling constable in the countryside was to arrange a 'meeting-point' in advance! The need for more efficient policing has also meant changes in organisation with the merger of police forces in Hull, the East Riding and Northern Lincolnshire to create the Humberside Police in 1974.

II

When Kilham was King

Growth and decline are facets of many parts of East Yorkshire with some towns and villages witnessing a rising tide of prosperity and population growth over the last two hundred years while other places have seen their fortunes wane. The village of Kilham, seven miles west of Bridlington, was once regarded as the capital of the Yorkshire Wolds with a thriving market and annual fairs but changes in transport in the later eighteenth century saw this ancient settlement lose out to nearby Driffield…

For those who rarely explore the quieter byways of East Yorkshire the village of Kilham, about five miles northeast of Driffield, might be unfamiliar. Yet diverting away from the busy A614 or B1249 routes soon brings you to one of the most picturesque places in the whole county. Situated in a valley amidst rolling hills Kilham extends about one-and-a-quarter miles from east to west with a wealth of houses and cottages from the eighteenth and nineteenth centuries. At the heart of the village is All Saints' church dating back to Norman times. Writing in 1823 the journalist Edward Baines described it as 'large and lofty' and expressed the opinion that it 'seems to have been designed for a more numerous congregation than the present population of the parish can supply.'

The size and splendour of All Saints' is testament to the wealth and importance of Kilham in the Middle Ages for by the late thirteenth century the Market Place in front of the church was attracting produce from a wide area. In 1227 a royal charter was granted for a market on a Tuesday and for a two-day fair in August and in 1334 these rights were extended to include another fair in November. The fairs and markets brought together buyers and sellers providing a range of livestock, food and merchandise including horses, sheep, cheese, shoes, caps and hardware. Such large gatherings of people also brought the potential for disorder and from court records in the East Riding Archive we learn of disturbances at Kilham on 1 November 1721. Joseph Lonsborough, a farm labourer from Foxholes, was accused with others of taking part in a riot and of assaulting a constable.

As a market town Kilham must have been a lively bustling place attracting a range of tradesmen and by the eighteenth century there were weavers, a glazer, a mechanic, a watchmaker, surgeons and other skilled workers plying their trades. Another notable industry was rope making which existed from the early eighteenth century until the late 1930s while, in common with other East Riding settlements, the village could rely on the services of its own miller. By the mid-nineteenth century the windmill stood in the south of the village and part of its tower can still be seen in Millside.

Like all villages of the time however the main industry of Kilham was agriculture and a directory of 100 years ago lists over thirty farmers. Other tradesmen too, like blacksmiths, were dependent on the farming industry for work like shoeing horses and repairing ploughs. By the mid-nineteenth century farming was more mechanised with steam-powered machinery in use for threshing corn. As local newspapers of the time show however this mechanisation sometimes led to accidents. In April 1864 an inquest was held in the village into the death of Robert Thirsk, a young man who died from his injuries after being caught in the moving parts of a steam threshing machine due to his carelessness.

Parts of Kilham's magnificent All Saints' church date from Norman times.

Those injured in such accidents were usually able to call the on the services of the village surgeon to attend to their wounds and in the case of Robert Thirsk he was seen by Thomas Atkinson, a doctor who also helped to run a private lunatic asylum in Kiham! In an age before antibiotics however he was not able to save his patient from the effects of blood poisoning when 'mortification took place.'

Atkinson himself died two years later and an obituary of March 1866 lamented the early death of a man who was the pioneer of 'every local movement having for its object the good of the village.' One of Atkinson's interests was education and he took a keen interest in the National School at Kilham. The building was erected in 1847 at a coat of £500 raised by local subscription and a grant from the Church of England's National Society. Atkinson's obituary claimed that the Kilham School owed 'much of its success to the late doctor.'

Such was the former importance of Kilham that it once had its own grammar school; in 1633 (during the reign of Charles I) it was endowed with sufficient funds to pay the schoolmaster his salary of £20 a year. In 1764 Kilham's grammar school was providing a free education to about thirty village children although by 1901 the school was 'in abeyance'. The former National School however continues in use to this day as Kilham Church of England Primary School and was described in the January 2007 OFSTED inspection report as an 'improving school providing a satisfactory standard of education.'

Interesting comparisons can be made, however, between the kind of school inspection reports made today with those of seventy years ago. In the 1920s and 1930s Kilham School was visited on numerous occasions by the local inspector of the East Riding County Council and his inspection reports (held by the East Riding Archive Service) show a kind of patronising arrogance that would be alien in today's educational climate. In November 1927, for example, the inspector reported:

Kilham Windmill with sails intact prior to 1950.

The new Headmaster has been here only a few weeks. He is young and enthusiastic, smart and energetic. Impressions are spoiled somewhat by his incessant praise of himself but probably he will become more sensible as he grows older.

The inspector seemed to develop a growing respect for this head teacher for in September 1936 he made some interesting comparisons with his replacement: 'He does not possess the strength of personality of his predecessor. I shall be surprised if his supervision of his assistants proves bracing and effective.'

During the same visit some of the teaching staff (who he described as a 'weak lot') received similar, abrasive, criticism. Of an elderly teacher nearing retirement he wrote:

I find much waste of time. The teacher is always very busy running here and there in a bewildered manner, talking all the time. The children rarely do anything useful and often through lack of suitable occupation are out of control.

Of course these forthright, insensitive and highly personalised comments were made decades before the Freedom of Information Act (2000) and it is unlikely that the teachers themselves ever saw the reports written about them!

The inspection findings of that time also point to the difficulties of teaching in a village primary school when educational budgets were tight. During a visit in February 1935 the inspector remarked on the poor heating from open fires in classrooms but a year later it seems central heating had at last been installed. He also pointed to the difficulties of two teachers 'handicapped by the fact that they share a classroom separated only by a curtain.'

Kilham's Church of England Primary School today. The school was originally built in 1847 for 380 children but in 1901 the average attendance was 115 boys and girls.

The Kilham Primary School of today, the resources available to it and the curriculum it offers are clearly far different from that of seventy years ago and in 2001 Kilham's results in reading and writing were in the top 5 per cent of schools nationally. Margaret Stow moved to Kilham from Hull fifteen years ago and said of her decision to settle in the village: 'I moved here for the schools. My daughter attended Kilham Primary School and then moved on to Driffield School for her secondary education. She is now eighteen and is hoping to go to university.' She went on to explain the appeal of Kilham in these terms: 'Village life is completely different to Hull. The community spirit in Kilham is excellent and the activities that take place at our village hall make the village a friendly, close-knit place to live.'

The Kilham of today also benefits from its relative isolation from Driffield in that it has retained shops and businesses that might otherwise have been closed by the chill wind of competition. With a motor garage in Chapel Lane, Kilham Stores, two public houses, a post office and a butcher's shop Kilham has fared better than many other villages in the East Riding. Peter Harrison has lived in Kilham for forty-seven years and since 1960 has been operating the village butcher's shop. He said of his business:

This was a butcher's shop before I took over and there was also an abattoir here until about fourteen years ago when increasing health and hygiene regulations made it difficult to continue with that side of the business. I have found that the people of Kilham, particularly the older generation, are very supportive of local businesses.

In the long term Kilham suffered a decline from its former importance because of the rise of Driffield after the construction of the Driffield Canal in 1770. A market was still held in Kilham as late as 1792 but by 1823 Edward Baines recorded that it was now 'wholly disused'. Kilham's fairs lasted longer but they too had gone by 1888. Yet although Kilham may have had to surrender the title of 'Capital of the Wolds' to its larger rival, much remains in this attractive settlement to remind today's visitors of its glorious past.

12

Trouble on the Tracks

In an age of ever-increasing car ownership and at a time when most goods are moved by road transport it is not surprising that the death toll on the country's roads has seen a rapid increase. By comparison railways have long been seen as a safer mode of transport although, as the ten fatalities of the Great Heck rail crash (Selby) showed in February 2001, no method of moving people or goods can ever be risk free. When the rail network was far larger than it is today (before the Beeching Cuts of the 1960s) accidents were more common and this was as true of East Yorkshire as other any other part of the United Kingdom…

From the moment that railways began accidents became a feature of this revolutionary form of travel. The first 'celebrity' casualty was the MP William Huskisson who was knocked down and killed by the *Rocket* during the opening ceremony of the Liverpool & Manchester Railway in September 1830. Part of the problem was that passengers paid little heed to the dangers of rail travel and clambered in and out of railway carriages in the same way as they had with stagecoaches. A railway guide, published in 1838, warned passengers to get in and out of the train on the left side to prevent being 'knocked down by a passing train.'

From 1840 the government began to take more interest in safety matters and the Railway Inspectorate of the Board of Trade was established to look into railway accidents and make recommendations on avoiding them in the future. Their first inspection was carried out in 1840 into an accident at Howden in East Yorkshire. On 7 August 1840 a train on the Hull & Selby Railway was derailed when a large cast-iron casting en route from Leeds to Hull fell from a truck immediately behind the locomotive. As a result of the derailment four people in the sixth carriage of the train were killed instantly or died later of their injuries. The Railway Inspectorate found that the casting (part of a weighing machine to be used at Hull station) had been insecurely fastened and made recommendations about the transport of such loads in future.

The inspector's report also contains details of a second accident on the Hull & Selby Railway only a month later, although this time there was no loss of life. This accident happened on 7 September 1840 at the Hull terminus (then at Kingston Street, close to the Humber Dock). The report indicates the scant regard paid to the safety of passengers at that time for the driver of the locomotive had been told to detach it from the rest of the train while it was still in motion and run it into a siding while the carriages continued under their own impetus to the platform! The Board of Trade report indicates graphically what happened next: 'This impetus, however, being too great the train continued its course until the foremost carriage containing several passengers ran against and broke through the end wall of the station.'

One man had his thigh broken by the impact, one lost three fingers of his left hand while other passengers and the guard were 'bruised and otherwise slightly injured.' The accident was remarkable in that the guard, John Smith, told the enquiry that he thought it was inevitable since the locomotive was detached only 500yds from the terminus and none of the carriages had any brakes to slow their speed, estimated at 20-25mph!

A busy station in Victorian times. The potential for accidents was heightened by the public's unfamiliarity with railways and unsafe practices such as piling luggage onto the roofs of carriages. (This 1862 painting, *The Railway Station*, is by William Frith.)

The opening of the Hull to Bridlington Railway in 1846 was soon to lead to other accidents, sometimes caused by staff carelessness. In 1852 a runaway locomotive knocked down several people gathered on the Beverley station level crossing while in 1865 a young man (who was probably drunk at the time) jumped out of a train approaching Driffield station to retrieve his hat! He survived the fall but had to receive medical attention for leg fractures.

Mechanical failures on the trains themselves sometimes led to injury. A report in the *Driffield Times* from 23 April 1864 recorded a serious accident north of Lockington when a defective wheel on the first carriage of the train led to the floor being 'split in two by violence from beneath'. Prior to this the jolting of the carriage had become so severe that three passengers, fearing for their lives, had leapt from the train. One received head injuries, another a broken leg and the third a twisted ankle. This early morning train, from Hull to Driffield (packed with butchers and cattle dealers attending Driffield Market), was eventually brought to a halt a mile from Hutton Cranswick station before any of the other forty passengers in the carriage could leap from it.

Accidents to railway workers were also a feature of the times and in 1861 a train killed the gatekeeper at Flemingate level crossing in Beverley. In May 1877 an inquest was held on another employee of the North Eastern Railway, Edward Beall, a joiner working on the line between Hutton Cranswick and Driffield who had been run over and decapitated by a goods train. Although there was some suggestion by the coroner that the driver was not paying enough care and attention the jury returned a verdict of 'accidental death'.

As the East Riding's network of railways expanded so too did the accidents. By the late 1860s there were lines linking Hull to Withernsea and Hornsea aiming to develop both places as seaside resorts. The twenty-mile-long railway line to Withernsea (known as the Hull & Holderness Railway) opened on 27 June 1854 and served places like Hedon and Patrington along its route.

During the busy summer months with excursion trains from Hull and the West Riding any mishap could cause serious disruption since this was a single-track railway. The *Hull Times* of Saturday 1 September 1866 recorded an accident the previous evening when the 8 p.m. train from Hull was derailed east of Hedon station resulting in a complete blockage of the line. When news of the accident reached Withernsea the large numbers of excursionists there were thrown into panic and all the available cabs, carriages and other vehicles were pressed into service to get them back to Hull. Many had to stay in Withernsea all night since there was not enough transport to get them home.

Less than a week later the line was blocked again when on 5 September the 7.45 p.m. train was derailed between Marfleet station and Hedon after a collision with a horse. The engine and tender ended up in a field and the first carriage was thrown onto its side. Miraculously the only casualty was the engine driver who was 'slightly cut about the face by the coke which was thrown about in all directions.'

Another line built in the 1860s was that from Beverley to Market Weighton and York. By 1890 Market Weighton was also joined to Driffield by a double-track railway serving country villages like Middleton-on-the-Wolds and Bainton. Coal trains from the West Riding also used the route and in December 1892 one of these smashed through the level crossing gates at Kellythorpe (near Driffield), it was claimed, because the driver mistook the signal.

One of the accident 'blackspots' of railways in East Yorkshire was Hull's Paragon station. Opened in May 1848 and replacing the earlier Hull station at Kingston Street this terminus grew to cover some two and a half acres. Hull Paragon was where three major routes joined: those from Selby and Doncaster to the west, those from Beverley, Bridlington and Scarborough in the north and those serving Hornsea and Withernsea in the east. By 1924 Hull's Paragon station was also serving passengers on the former Hull & Barnsley Railway too. The complexities of the track layout, points and signalling at Paragon station might help to explain the eight accidents that occurred there in the period from 1880 to 1929.

One of the most serious of these took place on 14 February 1927 at around 9.10 a.m. when an incoming passenger train from Withernsea collided head-on with an outgoing Scarborough train. The telescoping of coaches led to serious loss of life with twelve passengers killed and twenty-four suffering serious injuries. Two months after the accident an official report concluded that one of the signalmen had, by mistake, moved the wrong set of points diverting the Scarborough train onto the wrong track. His error was perhaps understandable in that three signal boxes controlled the railway lines into and out of the station with a total of 442 levers to operate!

The inspector seems to have believed that a contributory factor in the disaster of 1927 was the fact that the Withernsea train was already ten minutes late, and that the signalmen, not wishing to delay it further, acted in haste and were careless. He attached no blame to the enginemen of either train for in each case the signals were set in their favour. In the case of the Withernsea train he said that any view they might have had of the approaching Scarborough train was obscured by the curvature of the track. Interestingly, although twelve people died in this tragedy no one faced any charges of manslaughter.

The closure of the Hull to Withernsea and Hull to Hornsea routes in October 1964 and the Beverley to York route in November 1965 meant that Paragon station in Hull became less busy and perhaps safer as a result. There were economies too on lines that remained open with the closure of less-used stations. One of these was Lockington station on the Hull to Bridlington route. It closed on 13 June

The head-on collision between an incoming Withernsea train and an outgoing Scarborough train near Paragon station, Hull on the 14 February 1927. A signalman had mistakenly switched the Scarborough train onto the wrong track.

The aftermath of the Lockington train crash of 26 July 1986. A van driver drove his vehicle onto the ungated level crossing and this was struck by the 9.33 a.m. Bridlington to Hull train. In the derailment that followed nine people were killed and fifty-nine injured. The remains of the Ford Escort van lie by the side of the track while in the distance is the wreckage of the train. (courtesy of Bill Fussey)

1960 but twenty-six years later became the location of another serious accident. On 26 July 1986 the 9.33 a.m. Bridlington to Hull train hit a van on the ungated level crossing near to the station and was derailed. The 'lights-only' crossing had replaced manually operated gates six months earlier as part of economy measures to stop the line from being closed. Following the collision the front coach of the train overturned, the second ended up on the opposite track and the others were derailed leaving nine people dead and fifty-nine injured.

The subsequent enquiry into the Lockington rail crash found that the signals had been working correctly and that the van driver had driven onto the crossing by mistake. It also raised serious issues about the safety of this type of remotely monitored level crossing with the result that it was decided to install barriers at all crossings on the line by the end of 1988.

Despite the loss of life and injury on the once extensive East Riding rail network it would be easy to exaggerate the dangers of this form of travel. In the early days of railways it is clear that important lessons on safety still had to be learned since dangerous working practices resulted in death and injury. The travelling public also had to adjust to this new form of transport and recognise that they had to take some responsibility for their own safety. Yet however good the rules on rail safety became there always remained the problem of accidents caused by human error.

Map showing places served by railways in East Yorkshire by the 1950s.

13

Tough Times At North Newbald

Farming was once the mainstay of a host of East Riding villages with agriculture providing the main source of jobs both directly and though numerous supporting trades like blacksmiths and wheelwrights. Nowhere is this more evident than at the village of North Newbald eight miles west of Beverley and four miles south-east of Market Weighton. Here the trials and hardships of rural life (especially for the poor) are revealed in important evidence held by the East Riding Archive…

North Newbald is today one of the most picturesque places in the East Riding and archaeological evidence suggests that it has long been a popular place of habitation for the remains of a Romano-British villa were discovered nearby in the 1930s.

North Newbald lies in a sheltered hollow at the junction of three dales running down from the Yorkshire Wolds. The name Newbald, dating from Anglo-Saxon times, means 'new building' and the earliest documentary evidence about it comes from the tenth century. By the time of the Domesday Book (1086) the village was the property of the Canons of York and these churchmen continued to exert a powerful influence on North Newbald for the next 900 years. The most visible reminder of that presence is the magnificent church of St Nicholas replacing an earlier Saxon church on the same site.

Writing in 1892 the local historian J.G. Hall described the church of St Nicholas as 'the finest among the many fine parochial edifices in the East Riding' and it is easy to see why, for this building, dating from the twelfth century, has many interesting and original features. These include, on the south side, a doorway of five receding arches and above it a sculpted figure holding a book in his left hand and with his other hand raised in an act of benediction. Edward Baines wrote in 1823 'the figure is supposed to be one of the Priors.'

These powerful churchmen also secured a charter from King Edward III in 1348 granting a weekly market and annual fair at North Newbald and these were probably held on the village green. However, since this was the time of the Black Death, a disease that decimated up to a third of the population, it remains unclear how long Newbald's markets and fairs survived.

Until the late eighteenth century the lands around North Newbald were farmed communally under the open-field system but in 1783 an Act of Parliament began the process of enclosure with the scattered strips being reallocated to create separate farms. *Baines's Directory* of 1823 lists six 'farmers' at North Newbald but a further fourteen 'yeomen' who were generally men of respectable standing who farmed their own land (possibly under lease). Many more of the village's 543 inhabitants of that time would have been farm labourers or cottars with little or no land of their own working for these farmers and yeomen. The Enclosure Act of 1783 seems to have ushered in a period of great change at North Newbald with farmers building substantial new properties in the village at that time.

Unusually for an East Riding village many of these buildings were built from stone rather than the brick commonly used elsewhere. This hardwearing limestone came from quarries close by for Newbald stone was once a thriving industry and was used by medieval masons at Beverley for the building of St Mary's church and parts of Beverley Minster.

In the Domesday Book (1086) Newbald was recorded as being held by the Canons of York under Thomas the Archbishop. The great wealth of the church in medieval times helps to explain the splendour of North Newbald's own parish church, St Nicholas. It has been described as 'the most complete Norman church in the Riding'. A notable feature of the church is its south doorway with 'five receding arches and above it a sculpted figure holding a book in his left hand and with his other hand raised in an act of benediction.'

One of the stone-built structures in North Newbald itself is the old school erected by the Clough family in 1846. The log books of this Church of England school (held by the East Riding Archive) provide a fascinating perspective on life in the village over a century ago and indicate the vital importance of agriculture in the rural economy of the time. The log books read almost like a calendar of the farming year: on July 6 1863, for example, one entry says: 'School opened very thin. Turnip season commenced.'

In an age when school-attendance figures are usually seen as an important measure of a school's performance the frequent absences of nineteenth-century children (to undertake farm work) might seem shocking. However, for the poorer families of North Newbald work in the autumn was vital to ensure their survival over the winter months. Potatoes were an important part of the diet of the poor and on 24 October 1870 the schoolmaster was determined to justify the granting of leave of absence to his pupils in these terms: 'Many of the cottars have a small allotment of land in some ground devoted to that purpose called Canada and at this season of the year they are compelled to keep their children at home to assist in the potato harvest.' In June 1871 the link between the demands of farming and school attendance was once more revealed:

Reopened school with an attendance of just fifty. One farmer alone has engaged forty children to weed the corn. In consequence of the paucity of numbers I have thought it best to discontinue the regular work of the school as per the timetable.

The old village school was built by the Clough family in 1846. The school log books held by the East Riding Archive provide a fascinating day-by-day account of the problems of a rural village school at that time. The school was later moved to a site in Eastgate.

On 10 July came the decision to close the school for a week 'until there is less demand for fieldwork'. Part of the problem was that in 1870 elementary education was neither compulsory nor free. It was not until 1880 that schooling between the ages of five and ten was made mandatory and not until 1891 that the government provided enough funds to end the payment of fees. In any case some poorer families often needed the wages that a child could earn from tasks like singling turnips or gleaning (collecting leftover crops from fields after mechanical harvesting).

As the school log books show, it was not only farm work that disrupted the education of the children for there was also Market Weighton Fair and Cave Fair to distract them. Illness too played a part – and it was not only the pupils who were absent. On 2 May 1870 the log book records: 'In consequence of the Master being attacked by diptheria – school closed this week.'

A month later other entries record an outbreak of scarlatina (scarlet fever), a bacterial infection that was difficult to manage in the days before antibiotics. In any case since medical treatment had to be paid for in the late nineteenth century it would have been beyond the means of most Newbald parents to pay. The disease was characterised by a sore throat, fever and a rash over the upper body and for most people the only answer would have been to let the illness run its course. The log book, however, records the following events:

3 June 1870: Elizabeth Harland attacked with scarlatina.
6 June 1870: Elizabeth Harland died yesterday.
7 June 1870: Jane Lundy absent – attacked with scarlatina.

Like any other village in the Riding, life's misfortunes had to be met with fortitude by the poor of North Newbald for they had little alternative in the centuries before the creation of the 'Welfare State'. As a last resort there was poor relief from the parish either in North Newbald's own poor house (with accommodation for four paupers) or by means of 'outdoor relief' to paupers living in their own homes. The accounts of the overseers of the poor for North Newbald in 1798 show payments of 4s a week to the poorhouse for the upkeep of two paupers while another Newbald resident (Mark Tindle) was being paid by the parish at the rate of 2s a week for twenty-eight weeks. Whether his need to be supported by the parish was due to illness or some other cause is not known.

In one instance at least Newbald's overseers seem to have failed in their duty of care for on 10 July 1810 they were charged at the East Riding Quarter Sessions with 'refusing to pay adequate maintenance to Sarah Dales, a poor person of North Newbald, and her infant child Thomas Dales.'

In an age when bringing up a child outside of wedlock had both a social stigma attached to it and, before the advent of child allowances, a financial cost to the parish, becoming pregnant sometimes had dire consequences for poor women. On 18 December 1779 we learn of the voluntary examination of Mary Todd of North Newbald, single woman, taken under oath before a magistrate. She told him that: 'she is now with child and that the said child is likely to be born a bastard and to be chargeable to the township of North Newbald.'

Mary Todd then went on to tell the magistrate that the father of her unborn child was the labourer John Stather, late of Swanland. Presumably she did this so that the authorities, in order to avoid paying her themselves, could exert pressure on Stather to pay maintenance.

Back-breaking manual toil in the fields. *The Gleaners* by Jean-Francis Millet 1857. (courtesy of Musée d'Orsay, Paris)

North Newbald of the past: the wheelwright shop of Joseph Levitt around 1900.

For those who were deemed able to work but did not (and therefore were seen as a burden on the poor rates) life could be made very unpleasant. From court records in the East Riding Archive we learn of the conviction of Ann Clough who had: 'Wilfully neglected to maintain herself so she has become chargeable to the parish of North Newbald'. For this offence the unfortunate woman was sentenced to three months imprisonment (with hard labour) in the Beverley House of Correction.

Rough justice could also be meted out to those villagers who resorted to poaching in order to supplement a meagre diet. A quarter sessions file of 20 October 1830 records a fine of £5 on William Raspin of North Newbald for 'killing game'. He had been caught by a local gamekeeper three days earlier using traps to catch rabbits.

According to the census returns from 1871 of the 360 people at work in North Newbald in that year 200 were directly engaged in farming. In the century and more since then, farming at North Newbald has undergone profound upheavals with periods of stagnation and decline, beginning with the Great Agricultural Depression around 1880 and also continuing into the 1920s and 1930s. Both during and after the Second World War farming was buoyant again, but with increasing mechanisation and rationalisation in more recent times farms are no longer as labour-intensive as they were a century ago.

14

Freedom Fighter

The year 2007 marked the bi-centenary of the abolition of the slave trade and this major human-rights landmark was celebrated in Hull by a £1.4 million programme of exhibitions, concerts and lectures. Other events included the release of the Hollywood blockbuster, Amazing Grace, *on the life of the Hull MP who championed the cause of freedom: William Wilberforce. In the struggle to end slavery no one has a greater claim to importance than Hull's most famous son...*

Many visitors to Hull's historic High Street will have seen its famous Wilberforce House, the first museum in Britain to deal with the subject of slavery and the fight for its abolition. Opened in 1906 the museum has recently undergone a transformation with new displays on the history of slavery and the role of William Wilberforce in its abolition.

Wilberforce House was in fact the birthplace of the famous abolitionist. He was born here on 24 August 1759, the third child and only son of Robert Wilberforce, a prosperous Hull merchant. Although his father died when he was only nine the young William must have had a fairly privileged childhood; he was educated first at Hull's sixteenth-century grammar school, later as a boarder at Pocklington School (1771-1776) and then at Cambridge University. By the time he left William was extremely wealthy, having inherited substantial sums from both his grandfather and a childless uncle, and this may have influenced his decision to pursue a political career. Any politician in the eighteenth century needed a large fortune for parliamentary electioneering was both a tough and expensive business. When he was barely twenty-one William stood for election in Hull (1780) and his riches would have been vital to secure the 1,129 votes needed for victory since most voters expected to be bribed for their support! Four years later he became MP for the even more expensive county seat of Yorkshire while his friendship with another Cambridge graduate, William Pitt the younger (who became Prime Minister in December 1783), seemed to herald a promising political career. Yet following a sudden conversion to Evangelical Christianity in 1785 Wilberforce determined to dedicate the remainder of his life to the service of God and to 'moral causes'.

Chief among these was the abolition of the slave trade. The story is told of a conversation between Pitt and Wilberforce under an oak tree at Holwood in Kent (May 1787) when the Prime Minister urged Wilberforce to make the cause of abolition his own.

For decades the 'triangular trade' had been a feature of Britain's growing maritime commerce. Slaving boats left Britain for the west coast of Africa where guns and other manufactured goods were traded for African slaves. These slaves were then transported in the most appalling inhumane conditions, and at great loss of life, to the Americas for work on the plantations. Products like sugar, tobacco and cotton would then be shipped back to Britain making the merchants of Bristol and Liverpool extremely wealthy in the process.

Drawing on the evidence amassed by anti-slavery campaigners like Thomas Clarkson, Wilberforce became the foremost champion of the anti-slave trade movement in the House of Commons. During a long speech on the 12 May 1789 he pointed to the horrors of the slaving ships and the suffering of

Above left: The Wilberforce House Museum in High Street, Hull. The birthplace of William Wilberforce in 1759.

Above right: Still from the movie *Amazing Grace* about the life of William Wilberforce. (Murray Close © 2006 Bristol Bay Productions LLC; Ioan Grufford as William Wilberforce on the slave ship *Madagascar* in Michael Apted's *Amazing Grace*, a Samuel Goldwyn/Roadside Attractions Film).

Slave labour under the plantation system in the Americas (from a nineteenth-century painting).

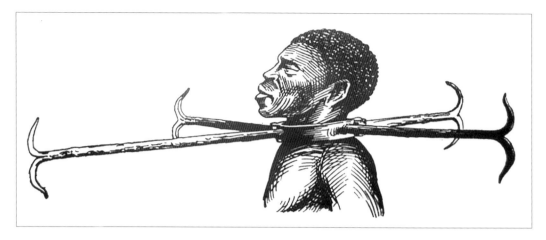

A collar designed to stop slaves escaping.

their human cargoes in the cramped conditions below decks during the two to three months of the Middle Passage; it is said that a slaving ship could be smelt from many miles away.

Large numbers of slaves did not survive the voyage and in some cases the dead and the dying were simply thrown overboard. Despite the power of Wilberforce's arguments there were many MPs who argued that more evidence was needed before any responsible decision could be taken on the slave trade and it would take a further eighteen years of campaigning before Wilberforce achieved success. It is a measure of his determination that he continued with the struggle despite numerous setbacks: his house in Westminster became a centre for the abolitionists and in January 1790 he persuaded Parliament to set up a select committee to examine the evidence on the slave trade. Yet when he tried to bring in legislation the following year his moves were rejected by the House of Commons. The outbreak of the French Revolution in 1789 and of a slave rebellion in Haiti in early 1791 made many MPs nervous of change.

Although Wilberforce remained optimistic about the cause of abolition there were powerful vested interests pitted against him. Some politicians even praised the slave trade on the grounds that it encouraged the development of Britain's merchant fleet and was, in their words, 'the nursery of seamen'. Although an Abolition Bill was passed in 1792 the inclusion of the words 'gradual abolition' meant that the new law was meaningless in real terms. Wilberforce's campaigning also led to personal danger for he had accused a slave-ship captain, John Kimber, of having flogged a slave girl to death. Kimber pursued Wilberforce both for an apology and compensation and even threatened him with physical violence.

The outbreak of war against France and the delaying tactics of the powerful West Indies lobby meant there was little progress in the 1790s and though Wilberforce continually reintroduced his Abolition Bill every year it was rejected. The turning point in the campaign came in the early nineteenth century with the arrival of more MPs in favour of abolition (especially from Ireland after 1801) and the publication of a new book by Wilberforce (January 1807) restating the horrific evidence against the slave trade that had been gathered in the preceding decades. When a new Abolition Bill was passed by the House of Lords the Commons finally gave their support too. Glowing tributes were paid to Wilberforce and in a rare moment of praise his eighteen years of perseverance were rewarded with cheers from members of the House of Commons. Wilberforce's persistence had finally been successful in that the anti-slave trade bill passed the House of Commons by 283 votes to sixteen and became law on 25 March 1807. From now on British captains engaged in slaving were fined £100 for every slave found onboard their ships.

Despite the new law against the slave trade, slavery itself was not yet illegal; the issue remained of those who had already been sold into slavery. Despite his failing health Wilberforce continued to be

The Wilberforce Monument in Queens Gardens was first in erected 1834-1835 and moved to its present location in 1935.

an active campaigner in the fight to free these slaves. In 1823 the Anti-Slavery Society was formed and Wilberforce published an influential booklet in which he suggested that the emancipation of slaves was a matter of national duty to God. Poor health led to his resignation from Parliament in 1825 and although increasingly frail he lived long enough to see a bill for the abolition of slavery (with compensation for slave owners) passed by the House of Commons on 26 July 1833. As Wilberforce said: 'Thank God that I have lived to witness a day in which England is willing to give twenty million pounds sterling for the abolition of slavery.'

Three days later he was dead and, as befitting the high national regard for him, he was buried in Westminster Abbey. The presence at the funeral (3 August 1833) of so many MPs and peers was, in the words of *The Times*, 'testimony of the esteem in which he was held.' It seems that the people of Hull also shared this opinion for within a year of his death plans were in motion to erect a magnificent monument in his honour close to the western end of Queens Dock. When the dock was filled in a century later the statue of the emancipator in his senatorial robes was moved to the eastern end of Queens Gardens (1935).

There is little doubt that many people in Hull are as proud of its connection with Wilberforce today as they were at the time of his death over 170 years ago. His long-fought and hard-won campaigns, marked by this year's bicentenary celebrations, brought an end to the transatlantic slave trade and ultimately to the end of slavery in the British Empire of the time. However, one of the aims of the Wilberforce 2007 events is to raise awareness of the fact that slavery still exists in the guise of forced labour. It has been estimated that there are still 27 million slaves worldwide and one of the aims of today's campaigners is to eradicate modern-day slavery.

15

The Turbulent Life of Kay Kendall

One of the major attractions of the Holderness seaside resort of Withernsea is its famous 127ft-high lighthouse, built between 1892 and 1894. These days the lighthouse houses a museum dedicated to one of Withernsea's most famous daughters: the 1950s film star, Kay Kendall.

Although the tragically short life of 1950s film star Kay Kendall may have begun in Withernsea she was never really a permanent resident of the town. Her mother, the former actress Gladys Kendall (née Drewery), gave birth to Kay in the house of her parents on 21 May 1927 but her married home was in faraway London. Kay however returned to Withernsea with her mother on family holidays throughout her childhood and her first public appearance was made at the town's Bank Holiday Carnival in August 1932.

Kay Kendall came from a showbusiness background: her father, Terry, was a dancer and her grandmother, Marie Kendall, had been a famous music-hall star. Gladys Kendall pushed both Kay and elder sister Kim towards showbusiness careers and paid for them to have ballet lessons while their father taught them tap dancing. However, the stability of family life was undermined when Terry and Gladys divorced in the mid-1930s. Naturally rebellious, Kay's relationship with her mother was often strained and during her teenage years she would disappear to live with aunts after furious arguments. Tall and strikingly attractive by the age of twelve Kay Kendall could pass herself off as someone much older. With a brash self-confidence (on the surface at least) and an outlandish sense of humour she could be both forthright and outspoken. However, beneath this veneer of bravado Kay could display a vulnerable side to her character: she had an inferiority complex about her intellect and her appearance (especially her nose). Generous and extravagant to the point of foolishness she was often short of money and if she could not pay the rent flitted from place to place living out of cardboard boxes.

In spite of the drawbacks of being a Cockney chorus girl (as she described herself) she mixed easily with the rich, privileged and famous and by her mid-twenties had had a string of eligible suitors including Bill Hanson and James Sainsbury (both from wealthy business backgrounds), an English marquess and a Swedish prince (often seeing them concurrently!). Beautifully dressed in the latest fashions, Kay was a regular visitor to London's most famous restaurants and nightclubs and her beauty, outrageous behaviour and manic sense of humour made her a favourite of the party set. In real life Kay Kendall played the part of a drama queen to perfection. Those who knew her described Kay as gay, carefree and 'mad as a hatter!'

Kay Kendal was a woman who enjoyed shocking people with her outspokenness and once, in a loud voice, asked James Sainsbury during a meal in a crowded restaurant: 'Why is it James you only make love to me on Wednesday once a week?' It was this kind of mischievous and scandalous approach to life that endeared Kay Kendal to both friends and colleagues alike, while her sex appeal also helped to further her film career. This had begun around 1944 with work as a film extra at £5 a day in Ealing productions like *Champagne Charlie* and *Caesar and Cleopatra*. In the spring of 1945

Above left: Kay Kendall was born on the 27 May 1927 at Stanley House, Withernsea (in the shadow of Withernsea Lighthouse). The Withernsea Museum (at the lighthouse) was opened in 1989 by Dr Rolla and Kim Campbell (Kay Kendall's sister) as the Kay Kendall Memorial Museum. There is a video presentation of excerpts from Kay Kendall's films and other memorabilia. (courtesy of Paul Lakin)

Above right: Kay Kendall at about the age of ten. (courtesy of the Withernsea Lighthouse Museum)

Right: Kay Kendall at about age eighteen. Kay did much modelling work after the failure of the film *London Town*. (courtesy of the Withernsea Lighthouse Museum)

Kay Kendall was also due to appear as a lowly chorus girl in a new film being shot by J. Arthur Rank Studios called *London Town*. However, a passionate love affair between the eighteen-year-old actress and the fifty-six-year-old American director Wesley Ruggles helped to secure her elevation to one of the female leads in the film. When sister Kim pointed out that the American was already married Kay showed a typically cool indifference to the feelings of others by replying: 'Well that's just too bad. She found him first, but I'm here now.'

Although the affair eventually petered out, Kay Kendall's role in *London Town* did nothing for her long-term acting career. The film was a box-office disaster on its release in September 1946 and her professional fortunes languished in the doldrums for the next five years. A factor that helped to resurrect them was yet another affair conducted at the same time as her relationship with James Sainsbury. This time it was with the film producer Anthony Havelock-Allan, twenty-two years her senior and married to the actress Valerie Hobson. Havelock-Allan went so far as to divorce his wife in anticipation of marrying Kay but before this could happen she got 'cold feet' about the whole business.

It was the influence of Havelock-Allen, however, that helped to secure one of Kay Kendall's most famous film roles: that of Rosalind Peters in *Genevieve*. This film, released in 1953, is a light-hearted story about two couples taking part in the annual London to Brighton vintage car rally and was well received by critics, one of whom said that Kendall gave a 'cleverly judged comedy performance.' That the film turned out so well is testament to the professionalism of the cast and crew in that it was filmed in two months (October to November 1952), on a tight budget and in difficult weather. The talents of Kay Kendall as a comedienne are all the more remarkable when you consider that during the filming she took three days off to undergo an abortion (illegal at the time). The father was James Sainsbury and their relationship never really recovered from the trauma of this event.

In *Genevieve* Kendall played the part of Rosalind Peters. In this scene, set in a Brighton nightclub, she drinks too much champagne and gets up on stage to play the trumpet. The actual playing was done by accomplished musician Kenny Baker (also from Withernsea). (courtesy of Don Brockway)

Kay Kendall's gift for comedy – her timing and superb delivery of lines, her bemused half smile and cocked eyebrow (shown to good effect in *Genevieve*) – seemed to be a lesson lost on the Rank Organisation which proceeded to give her parts unsuited to her talents. Films like *The Square Ring* and *Abdullah the Great* did nothing for her career although in the latter she embarked on a new romance with her co-star, twenty-eight-year-old Sydney Chaplin, younger son of the legendary comedian of the silent era. In many ways the life of Kay Kendall herself was far more interesting and dramatic than the films she performed in!

Another turning point in Kay Kendall's life and career came in 1954 when got the part of the fashion photographer Monica Hendricks in the light comedy *The Constant Husband*. Her co-star was the accomplished forty-six-year-old actor Rex Harrison (nineteen years her senior) who had had a long career in films and had also gained a reputation as a notorious womaniser. From the outset Harrison was captivated by Kay. He was to describe her as: 'very easy, full of fun, flirtatious, impertinent and rakish'. Kay too was smitten by Harrison's charm and although their affair was to be a tempestuous one she had no intention of giving him up.

By 1954 Harrison had been married to the Polish-born actress Lilli Palmer for over ten years, but once Kay had a man in her sights she could be utterly ruthless in her pursuit of him. Obsessed with Harrison to the point of insanity she followed him to his family home in Portofino, Italy where a confrontation with Lilli Palmer ensued, sowing the seeds for divorce proceedings. The timing of the divorce was particularly unfortunate since Harrison and Palmer were due to appear together in the London stage production of *Bell, Book and Candle* (which cynics cruelly renamed Bell, Book and Kendall).

Kay Kendall was eventually to follow Harrison to New York where he had landed the role of Professor Henry Higgins in the Broadway production of *My Fair Lady*. The move to the USA was also good for her own career for Hollywood was to give her the kind of comedy roles she had long

Poster for the movie *Les Girls*, Kay Kendall's first American film (1957). (courtesy of MGM)

Kay Kendall with Broadway actor and film star Rex Harrison. The two appeared together in the 1958 film *The Reluctant Debutante*. Kay Kendall and Rex Harrison married in June 1957 after Harrison discovered that Kay was dying of leukaemia (a fact he tried to keep secret from her). (courtesy of the Withernsea Lighthouse Museum)

craved in England but had not been given. One of these films was *Les Girls* (1957) in which she was billed below Gene Kelly but effectively outperformed him with the kind of dizzy charm she was perfect for. The role in *Les Girls* helped to make her name in America and she even appeared as herself on television in *The Phil Silvers Show*.

The tragedy of Kay Kendall was that just as her comic genius had come to fruition her health began to deteriorate. She had been anaemic all her life but in January 1957 her doctor told Rex that she was suffering from leukaemia. Given the state of medical knowledge in the late fifties the diagnosis was effectively a death sentence. Harrison determined to keep the truth from her but also take care of her in the time she had remaining. The two were married in June 1957 and went on to star together in the film *The Reluctant Debutante* (1958). Although by now seriously ill she managed to complete one final film with Yul Brynner, *Once More With Feeling*, in June 1959. With Rex by her side, Kay entered a London clinic on 30 August and died there less than a week later.

The premature death of Kay Kendall at the age of just thirty-three robbed Britain of one of its brightest acting talents. It also robbed showbusiness of a star with a zest for life even if that life had been plagued by scandal and self-indulgence. Yet the story of Kay Kendall is also one of human frailties. At the height of her success Kay Kendall showed the same capacity for self-doubt that had plagued her in earlier times. During the summer of 1959 she told a reporter from *Life Magazine*: 'My feet are too big, my bosom is too small. I have huge hips and an enormous bottom. I can hardly breathe through this frightful nose. My hair looks like Danny Kaye in a wig.'

Although such comments could be dismissed as yet another 'performance' by a fine comedy actress, it seems that Kay Kendall genuinely believed what she was saying since she had told friends similar things. Yet, despite these misgivings about her appearance Kay Kendall possessed the drive, enthusiasm and above all the talent of a great comedy actress. The tragedy of the early death of the 'girl from Withernsea' was that she did not live to see that talent developed further.

16

A Violent Death at Bishop Burton

Situated in a sheltered hollow astride the A1079 road from Beverley to York, Bishop Burton has long been regarded as a picture-book English village with its neat whitewashed cottages, two village ponds, a charming church and an unhurried pace of life. Back in 1909 however this sleepy community became the focus of unwelcome attention after a violent death at harvest time…

One of the major trends in East Yorkshire farming during the twentieth century has been increasing mechanisation. A hundred years ago agriculture was far more labour intensive than it is today and there was a need for casual labour, particularly at harvest time. The farms around Bishop Burton and other Yorkshire Wolds villages therefore saw an influx of workers from Ireland and other parts of the United Kingdom. They often slept rough in barns and outhouses and at Gardham Farm, west of Bishop Burton, the farmer had employed a number of such men as 'harvesters' during September 1909.

Since Sunday was a day of rest four of these men had decided, on the afternoon of 19 September, to walk from their farm to the nearest public house: the Altisidora in Bishop Burton. The four were James Fee and James Murray (both from Ireland) together with Edward Dunn and his cousin Arthur Ashworth from Burnley in Lancashire. A considerable number of harvest men (including some from Lings Farm in Bishop Burton) had gathered at the Altisidora by Sunday evening and after drinking several pints of beer the Gardham men had become noisy and troublesome to the landlord, particularly the twenty-five-year-old James Fee. At around 10 p.m. he asked Fee to leave. The four drunken men then left the Altisidora and were confronted by the local policeman, PC Hodgson. He was later to assert that Fee was quarrelsome, foul-mouthed and aggressive. It would seem that the four men then walked out of the village for their journey back to the farm at Gardham.

In the early hours of Monday morning Hodgson was contacted at his home in nearby Cherry Burton to say that a body had been found in the road about a mile from Bishop Burton. The corpse was that of Edward Dunn and at a subsequent inquest a local doctor described his injuries. These included a contusion over the right eye, swelling to the lower eyelid, and bruising to the forehead and face. However, the cause of death was a fractured skull caused, the doctor thought, when Dunn, under a sustained assault, had fallen backwards and had struck his head on the road. Hodgson was to claim that during a search of the area near the body he had found James Fee asleep and that Murray was also close by. Both men were arrested at the scene while Arthur Ashworth was apprehended some hours later at Gardham Farm. All three men were charged with causing the death of Edward Dunn and appeared before East Riding magistrates on Monday 20 September.

For the three accused men part of their problem was that they could not afford legal assistance and so were not represented in court. Being simple ill-educated labourers they were unlikely to have been able to defend themselves. From the outset assumptions seem to have been made about the guilt of Thomas Fee based on the evidence of his drunken behaviour at the Altisidora, his swearing and his eagerness to be involved in a fight. PC Hodgson's judgement may have been clouded by his unpleasant encounter with Fee earlier and perhaps also by an anti-Irish prejudice. Hodgson

The Altisidora
public house
where harvesters
from farms
around the village
were drinking
on Sunday 19
September 1909.

was in fact well aware that that there had been other people present near the scene of the attack: Harry Gillbank, Charles Thornham and Michael McHugh, who were all employed at Lings Farm in Bishop Burton. However, instead of being seen as possible suspects in the case they were regarded as witnesses. The same prejudice against Thomas Fee can also be seen at the inquest into the death of Dunn held at the Beverley cottage hospital by Sir Luke White who had travelled from London to hear the case. At the inquest Fee had told the coroner that at the location where Dunn had been attacked three men had been lying in wait. One of the three, he claimed, was Harry Gillbank, a man he had argued with earlier at the Altisidora. Fee said that he had been so afraid of the three men that he had run away. Another of the accused, James Murray, corroborated Fee's story in that he told the coroner that he had seen Fee talking to Gillbank earlier at the Altisidora.

Yet instead of declaring an adjournment so that the police could investigate further the coroner chose to suggest that Fee's evidence was untrustworthy and that the circumstances of Dunn's death indicated manslaughter or wilful murder. The coroner then suggested to the jury that there was a case against Fee and after thirty minutes deliberation they arrived at the incredible conclusion, on the flimsiest of evidence, that Fee had committed manslaughter but that Murray and Ashworth were not responsible. However, all three men remained in custody and on Saturday 25 September were brought from Hull Prison to Beverley for another hearing before East Riding magistrates. They were again remanded in custody with their next appearance set for the following Thursday.

In the light of the coroner's inquest and with the odds stacked against them it easy to see how a miscarriage of justice might now have occurred. That it did not owed something to the decision of the police to reopen their investigations after two of the 'star' witnesses at the inquest, Harry Gilbank (aged twenty-one and from Flamborough) and Charles Thornham (aged seventeen and from Hull), failed to turn up for the committal proceedings on 25 September. The following day PC Hodgson, accompanied by his superior officer Sgt Peckitt, went to Lings Farm at Bishop Burton and arrested the pair.

Sensational developments, fully reported in the *Beverley Guardian* of the time, then followed. At Beverley police station Thornham was interrogated and gave a statement that incriminated Gilbank in the killing of Edward Dunn. From his evidence, and that of Michael McHugh (also employed at Lings Farm as a 'harvester'), it seems that there had been a drink-fuelled quarrel between Harry Gilbank and James Fee at the Altisidora and that this had 'spilled' outside! Gilbank was eager, it was said, to settle scores and he and his accomplices had armed themselves with sticks and lay in wait for Fee and the others. Yet it was Gilbank who, according to the others, was spoiling for a fight and launched the attack. According to Michael McHugh, Gilbank had dashed out into the road and had struck one man on the head while the other had 'run off like lightning'. In the darkness and confusion however it seems that Gilbank had chosen the wrong man to attack!

In the light of Thornham's statement the charges against Fee, Murray and Ashworth were then dropped and the three men released. However, Arthur Asworth's troubles were not over, for the publicity surrounding his arrest in East Yorkshire came to the attention of the Burnley police. On his return home he was arrested, charged with deserting his wife and children and sentenced to two months imprisonment with hard labour.

On 9 October 1909 Thornham too was released, leaving only Harry Gilbank to face trial at York Assizes in November 1909. Given the catalogue of errors that had already been made in the case the Beverley magistrates now committed another error of judgement in sending Gilbank to trial on an inappropriate charge: that of wilful murder. Based on the evidence of his would-be accomplices it would seem that Gilbank had planned an attack on Fee rather than Dunn and that Dunn's death had been something of an accident. It would therefore have been more appropriate to charge Gilbank with manslaughter. This was referred to by Mr Justice Bucknill on 20 November 1909 when he said he was 'unable to understand why the magistrates at Beverley had committed the accused for trial on the capital charge.'

In the event Gilbank was a very fortunate individual because when the judge invited the Grand Jury to reduce the charge to one of manslaughter they declined to do so, with the result that Gilbank did not have to face trial at all. Mr Justice Bucknill neatly summed up the surprise of everyone at the York Assizes when he declared: 'it was the most extraordinary case he had ever heard during twelve years on the Bench.'

Thus, the death of Edward Dunn may be seen as a crime that went unpunished largely due to the incompetence of the authorities. Having falsely accused Thomas Fee of the crime they then brought in the wrong charge against the man who seems to have been responsible: Harry Gillbank. In releasing Gillbank from custody however the judge pointed to the real culprit in the tragic death of Dunn: alcohol. It seems clear that the excessive amount of beer that was drunk in the Altisidora on 19 September 1909 was a major factor in the events that followed.

The road to the beautiful village of Bishop Burton today.

17

Health Care Before the NHS

In the twenty-first century we often take for granted the provision of free health care under the National Health Service. However, before July 1948 many of the less well off were deterred from seeking medical help because of the costs they would incur. The creation of the Welfare State meant, for the first time, the government took responsibility for all medical services including free diagnosis and treatment in hospitals…

One of the more interesting aspects of history is the way in which the meaning of words has changed over the centuries. The word hospital, for example, once suggested a place of refuge for needy people (like Ann Routh's Hospital, for widows, in Beverley's Keldgate, founded in 1746). It was only with improvements in medicine that a hospital's modern-day association with the treatment of the sick became more apparent; to avoid confusion these newer institutions were often called infirmaries or dispensaries.

One thing in common between the old usage of the word hospital and its newer meaning was the dependence of both on charity. The first infirmaries and dispensaries were charitable institutions funded by bequests from wealthy benefactors and by subscribers who nominated or recommended poor patients. A Beverley dispensary was established as early as 1817 using a charitable bequest left by William Wilson and by 1828 had moved into a new building in Register Square. It continued to supply medicines to out-patients who otherwise would not have been able to afford them and fifty years later was joined by a facility for in-patients, the cottage hospital, run on similar lines. The Beverley cottage hospital at first used a house in Norwood for its work and there were beds for just seven patients.

In the early years the hospital seemed to have problems retaining staff and from a minute book in the East Riding Archive we learn that in April 1883 a new matron was being sought at 'a salary of £30 a year.' Of the twenty-seven applicants for the job three were called for interview with the post being awarded to Miss Jane Henderson, a nurse from a workhouse infirmary in East Middlesex. Unfortunately her tenure as matron was to last only a few months since on 18 October 1883 she resigned 'on account of her approaching marriage'. In Victorian times, and long after, marriage was usually seen as a bar to further employment. However, perhaps wracked by guilt at her short stay or motivated by family loyalty she then proposed her sister, Charlotte, a nurse at Islington Infirmary in London, as her replacement!

In the event Charlotte Henderson declined to attend an interview and the post had to be readvertised in *The Lancet* and *The Medical Times*. It was not until 1 December 1883 that the new matron, Nurse Bates from Leeds, took up her post but she only stayed for two years. Her salary may have been an issue for on 10 February 1885 she had asked for a pay rise but had been told that 'that the application was premature.'

The financial problems of running a voluntary hospital when the only income came from donations, bequests, subscriptions and 'fundraising' must have been painfully obvious to the managing committee. The minutes of their meetings are full of gratitude to the organisations and individuals

Keldgate, Beverley. Before hospitals or infirmaries took on a medical role they often provided shelter for the old or infirm.

making gifts as, for example, on 8 January 1884 when the members of the Hull Gymnasium were thanked for their 'entertainment given in aid of the hospital' and which raised £5 4s.

In order to make more efficient use of the charitable bequests that were available it is not surprising that by April 1883 a merger between the dispensary and the cottage hospital was being proposed. Two years later a joint committee of the two were considering plans for a new dispensary and hospital to be built on a site in Morton Lane, Beverley. After looking at drawings supplied by various architects they opted for the designs of Smith and Brodrick of Hull and the plain red-brick building they recommended took shape and was opened in 1886. A local newspaper recorded the philanthropy of prominent people of the time in supporting the new venture with Lord Hotham donating £50 and the local tannery business of Richard Hodgson and Sons providing a further £100 towards the cost of the building (estimated to be around £1,900).

Civic pride and charitable instincts were also powerful motives in other East Riding towns eager to establish their own cottage hospitals. The *Driffield Times* of 22 December 1886 records the first tentative steps taken in that town to enlist support for the project and indicates the way the subscription system worked: 'Every subscriber of one pound will be entitled to recommend one in-patient and two out-patients but as the number of beds is limited, the cases must be admitted according to their urgency and the probability of cure'.

In the case of the six-bed Driffield cottage hospital, established in temporary accommodation on Eastgate in 1867, the driving force was Mary Sykes of Sledmere and Elizabeth Reynard of Driffield and by 1871 the managing committee had begun raising funds for a purpose-built hospital (opened in 1873).

Plans for the new cottage hospital, Morton Lane, Beverley, drawn up by Hull architects Smith & Brodrick of Hull in 1885. The new hospital opened a year later. (courtesy of the East Riding Archive Service)

Not to be outdone Bridlington soon followed suit. Early in 1868 a newspaper recorded that 'a lady deeply interested in the welfare of the town has offered a large sum of money to establish a dispensary.' The lady in question was Alicia Maria Lloyd who wanted to endow a memorial to her mother by providing £1,200 for a dispensary to benefit 'the industrious and deserving poor'. As a temporary measure a building on Quay Road was purchased for £120 to serve as a hospital while the first meeting of subscribers took place on 16 May 1868. By August of that year the hospital was ready to carry out its first operation: a local surgeon removed, without anaesthetic, a cancerous tumour from the face of Arthur Myles, a Bridlington fisherman. Accounts from 1869 show that the income from subscriptions was just over £138 and in common with most cottage hospitals extra funds were generated through events like charity balls, bazaars, church collections and garden parties.

Plans were soon in hand for a purpose-built hospital and, like Beverley cottage Hospital, Smith & Broderick of Hull produced the designs for the building. Opened in April 1876 the Lloyd cottage hospital provided fifteen beds but within twenty years an extension was built to provide more accommodation.

From reports in local newspapers and from occasional references in the minute books of the managing committees we can get some idea of the work of cottage hospitals. Like the modern-day work of accident and emergency departments, cottage hospitals believed that dealing with serious injury was a priority. As a report in the *Driffield Times* stated in reference to the proposed cottage hospital in the town: 'Cases of accident will be received at once without any recommendation, provided that a bed be at liberty at the time.'

A newspaper report of 18 November 1876 shows how this principle was put into practice for one admission to the hospital was a six-year-old child called Arthur Jennison from the village of Cranswick. He had been standing too close to the fire at home and his shirt had caught alight. The boy died from his horrific injuries less than a week after being admitted. Another report in the *Driffield Times* for 21 August 1886 reveals how a farm labourer, James Briggs, had been badly injured falling out of a train on the Malton to Driffield line. After admission to the Driffield cottage hospital his injured arm, smashed near the elbow, was 'amputated by Doctors Wood, Burgess and Bell.'

The development of transport and industry at Beverley also provided more patients for the new cottage hospital. On 2 October 1890 the clerk to the directors was asked to write to Colonel Vickers of Sheffield with regard to one of his employees, a boilermaker, who had died at the hospital and to say that although no charges would be made he could, if he wished, make a donation. Meanwhile a minute of 5 March 1896 records a payment of 30s from the North Eastern Railway in respect of one of its servants, T.G. Nixon. In their letter to the hospital however the NER directors 'could not see their way to contribute an annual subscription.'

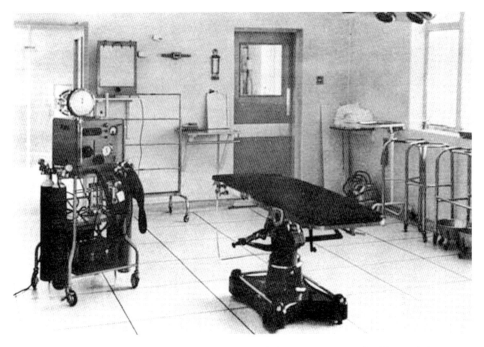

The operating theatre at the Lloyd Cottage Hospital. By 1900 surgeons had learned the importance of strict cleanliness and 'aseptic' techniques during operations.

Lloyd Hospital & Dispensary,

Quay Road, Bridlington.

Available to	No.

The Medical Officers attend on Wednesdays & Saturdays at 2-30 p.m. The Dispenser attends daily at 2-30 p.m., Sundays excepted.

193

I recommend

Residing at   *as an Out-patient*

of the Lloyd Hospital believing   *to be a proper*

object for this charity.

                                 Subscriber

This Ticket requires renewing at the end of one month from date when this ticket is presented. One Shilling to be paid

Ticket of recommendation. Before the NHS hospital treatment was not free. Wealthy subscribers were entitled to 'recommend' poor patients for treatment at the hospital.

THIS CAR CAN BE YOURS!

The accompanying photograph is a model of the Morris Eight Saloon Car, Series I., in blue, with blue upholstery, which has been given by Mr Gordon Armstrong, the well-known Beverley and Hull motor dealer, to help the funds of the Beverley Carnival and Shopping Week in aid of the Hospital.

This car, which is an absolutely up-to-the-minute production from the Morris works, combines all the valuable features of recent models with the latest innovations in the way of security, roominess, comfort, speed and action.

It does not differ in general design from a big car. It possesses a sound and exceptionally efficient four-cylinder water-cooled engine, with a totally enclosed three-speed synchromesh gear-box.

Special features of the car are its generous dimensions, hydraulic shock absorbers, hydraulic brakes, and rear axle of three-quarter floating type.

The car, which will be supplied complete with buffers front and rear, and electric traffic indicators, is valued at £128, and every person who fills in a coupon, selecting from 30 suggestions, the ten vegetables most suitable for hospital patients, stands an equal chance of winning this car for the outlay of a modest sixpence.

This Morris Eight is extremely economical to run, and its calls would not be beyond the poorest. The total road tax for the year is only £6, and the petrol consumption is just 45 miles to the gallon.

The car is capable of travelling at a speed of 60 miles an hour, and will seat four adults as comfortably as any bigger vehicle.

Coupons, which are priced at sixpence each, may be obtained from any of Messrs Gordon Armstrong's business establishments in Beverley or Hull, or from any member of the Carnival Committee. They should be filled in and returned as indicated on the coupon, where fuller particulars are also printed, as early as possible.

In the days before the NHS, fundraising by the local community helped to support cottage hospitals. Here is an advertisement from the *Beverley Guardian* of 1938 for a 'win-a-car' competition to help the funds of the Beverley Carnival in aid of the hospital. The Beverley industrialist Gordon Armstrong donated the prize, a Morris 8 car.

In the same year, 1896, the hospital became embroiled in a charge of negligence brought against the hospital dispenser, Mr Hind, by the Beverley firm of Cochrane & Cooper who built ships on the River Hull at Grovehill. The charge related to a young employee called Towse who first went to the hospital, on 17 August 1896, with an infected wound to his hand. According to the evidence presented to a special meeting of the directors Hind had refused to treat the wound himself but had told the patient to poultice it himself. When, within days, the boy's hand had turned black and he was in 'great pain', he had been seen by a doctor in the town whose opinion was 'the boy was in a dangerous state and that the arm had been neglected.'

On 4 September 1896, having heard the evidence presented on behalf of the patient and the denials of Mr Hind, the directors chose to dismiss the allegations. However, from subsequent events, it became clear the competence of Hind to do the job he was being employed for was now in serious doubt. Under an Act of Parliament of 1886 the rules on who could practice medicine and surgery had been made more stringent and it would seem that Hind lacked the necessary qualifications to carry out duties like dressing wounds. The opinions of the General Medical Council were sought in March 1898 and their view was that if Hind's duties were confined to dispensing medicines this would be acceptable, but working as a medical practitioner would not.

On 10 June 1898 the directors again met to discuss Hind's future at the hospital and although he was allowed to continue as the dispenser his salary was to be cut from £120 a year to £80. However, after some lobbying by Hind himself, he was finally awarded £100 a year (15 August 1898).

Until the creation of the NHS, cottage hospitals in the East Riding continued to rely on their subscribers, on gifts and on the fundraising activities of local supporters. As medicine progressed so the business of running a hospital became more expensive since new diagnostic tools, like x-ray machines, had to be bought. In 1918, at Lloyd's cottage hospital in Bridlington, the Holtby family of Rudston gave the hospital a complete and up-to-date set of x-ray equipment while a minute of March 1923 records the appointment of a Mr Brennen as honorary radiologist; it was agreed that he would receive half the fees paid by patients for their x-rays!

As before, fundraising occupied the ingenuity of hospital supporters and at the Lloyd cottage hospital a flag day on Hospital Saturday in August 1923 produced over £236. In Beverley, the coffers of their own cherished hospital were boosted by the support of Gordon Armstrong, a local industrialist, who donated a new Morris 8 saloon car for a competition held during the 1938 carnival week. Meanwhile in Driffield the generosity of Alfred Bean, a resident of Highfield, enabled the building of a new hospital on Bridlington Road and his name lives on through the modern-day facilities there.

There is little doubt that through voluntary effort the towns of the East Riding were able to provide the first real hospital services, however limited, in the modern sense of the word. With the creation of the NHS however came a movement for greater efficiency and in the long term smaller cottage hospitals were closed. The Lloyd cottage hospital closed in 1987 and was demolished in 1994 to make way for a supermarket. In Beverley plans to close the cottage hospital (by now a leading gynaecology hospital) were met with outrage. However, the protests were in vain and the site in Morton Lane closed in September 1991. The buildings were demolished to make way for housing.

While these actions were taken, it was said, to create more cost-effective and modern facilities such as those at the new Bridlington Hospital (opened 1987), at Castle Hill Hospital in Cottingham and at the Hull Royal Infirmary on Anlaby Road, the loss of 'community assets' supported by decades by voluntary effort has often been a cause of deep resentment.

18

Airships over East Yorkshire

The East Riding of Yorkshire has a long association with the history of flight and these days the factory of BAE Systems at Brough, on the banks of the River Humber, is still at the forefront of aeronautical innovation through its manufacture of the Hawk jet trainer. Another link in East Yorkshire's relationship with aviation history is that of airships, although here the underlying themes have been ones of tragedy and failure…

In an age when passenger travel across continents by jet aircraft is commonplace it is easy to forget that a century ago the future of powered flight by aeroplane was by no means certain. The Wright Brothers had made their first attempt at flying in a 'heavier-than-air machine' in 1903, but early planes tended to be unreliable and dangerous and flights in them of short duration. Other pioneers saw rigid airships filled with hydrogen gas as the way forward, notably the German aristocrat Count Zeppelin. Between 1900 and 1914 his work on airships gave Germany a head start over other European nations. When the First World War began in August 1914 the Germans had eight such Zeppelins and quickly built more. These new improved Zeppelins were capable of flying at 85mph and carrying 6 tons of bombs.

The first Zeppelin raids on Britain began in January 1915 with a raid on Great Yarmouth and Kings Lynn and on 16 June of that year Hull too became a target. For the local population who were only used to reading about warfare in their newspapers bombardment from the air was a new and terrifying experience. The attack by the Zeppelin L9 was recorded in some detail in the diaries of Hull resident George Thorp, who said:

> *At about 10pm the warning hooters sounded and I heard in quick succession three dull booming explosions in the distance. The damage to property is great, the loss of life severe. Incendiary bombs were dropped on the premises of Edwin Davis the draper and the whole of his premises in the Market Place has been reduced to ruins.*

At this stage in the war Hull was almost completely defenceless to this novel form of attack, the only response to the Germans coming from the guns of HMS *Adventure* under repair at Earle's Shipyard. With twenty-five people dead and damage to property severe, mobs of frightened people retaliated by attacking the shops of people they believed to be of German descent.

Other raids were to follow. On 9 August the L9 arrived at Aldborough on the Yorkshire coast, but due to navigational errors, the crew missed Hull and bombed Goole instead, killing sixteen people. Hull's next raid came in March 1916 when two Zeppelins hovered over the city for an hour dropping bombs on a shipyard and onto Hull railway station spectacularly destroying its glass roof. During this raid seventeen people were killed and sixty injured. In response to the pressure from local people and from Hull's MPs for some protection against the Zeppelin threat, an anti-aircraft gun was installed on the roof of Rose Down and Thompson's foundry. However, when it was discovered that this gun was a dummy one made out of wood, and there merely to appease public anger, there were further riots. Some Hull people took the only option they had when the 'buzzers' sounded and left the city for a night in the surrounding countryside.

Yet despite the initial poor response to the Zeppelin attacks the authorities began to make improvements to anti-aircraft defences and by bringing in fighter planes to drive off the German raiders. It was soon realised that the Zeppelin's hydrogen cells were vulnerable to the right kind of explosive shells and by 1917 seventy-seven out of their fleet of 115 ships had been brought down or disabled. The last raid on East Yorkshire came on 10 March 1918 when Zeppelin L63 arrived at Hornsea on the east coast and followed the railway line into Hull dropping bombs near Sutton and on Hull itself. Fortunately there was only one fatality.

The British military authorities too began to realise the growing importance of aerial warfare and in 1915 they sent two naval officers to find a suitable base from which airships could be used to protect shipping on the east coast from attack by German submarines. The site chosen was at Howden in East Yorkshire, where the Royal Naval Airship Station gradually took shape and opened in June 1916. Living accommodation, a large hydrogen gas plant and three airship sheds were just some of the facilities built here. One of these sheds was the largest in the world measuring 750ft in length and 130ft high!

In July 1921 the Howden airship station became the base for testing a new British airship, the R38, that had been bought by the United States Navy and who had shipped over some of their own personnel for training in how to fly it. The airship was the largest of its day: 695ft long and 122ft in diameter with a gas capacity of 2.7 million cubic feet. The design was a copy of the high-altitude wartime Zeppelins with a lightweight design that allowed a maximum performance to be achieved in thin air. Unfortunately no one had thought to calculate how it would handle in the denser air found at lower altitudes.

On Tuesday 23 August the airship carrying a crew of forty-nine (including seventeen Americans) set out from Howden on its fourth trial run. This took the R38 down to Norfolk, but by the next

The maiden flight of airship R38 from Cardington in Bedfordshire on 25 June 1921. The airship had been bought by the United States Navy and renamed the ZR-2. (courtesy of the Navy Historical Centre, Washington)

day it was back over the River Humber to undergo some low-altitude rudder tests; these were to simulate the kind of rough weather that might be expected over the Atlantic when the Americans were taking the ship home. In the event the tests proved too much for the fragile hull. At around 5.40 p.m. on 24 August witnesses standing on Hull Pier on the banks of the Humber and staring up at the silver cigar-shaped airship 2,500ft above their heads reported seeing creases in its fabric. Within seconds the R38 had broken in two; explosions swiftly followed as the hydrogen gas in the front section ignited. All forty-four members of the crew in that part of the airship were killed by a detonation of such intensity that windows over a large part of Hull's Old Town were shattered. The remains of the rear section however did not catch fire and plummeted into the River Humber. Rescue boats were quickly on the scene to give assistance but there were only five survivors. These included the captain, who was able to give evidence at the subsequent enquiry. This gave the cause of the disaster as structural weakness, although no attempt was made to delve deeper into the design failings of the airship. The enquiry seemed to ignore later suggestions that the designers had not paid any attention to the aerodynamic forces on the airframe. The structural weaknesses of the ship had only become evident with the kind of high-speed, low-altitude turn that had been attempted over the Humber.

The R38 catastrophe was greeted with stunned disbelief in Hull, at Howden and in the village of Elloughton (where four of the American officers had been living for some time before the tragedy). In the weeks that followed the funerals of the victims and memorial services attracted large crowds of East Riding folk anxious to pay their last respects. Many of the victims were buried in a mass grave at Hull's Western Cemetery where a monument to those who died still stands. Another memorial can be found in St Mary's church, Elloughton.

Seven of the would-be American crew of the R38 en route to Great Britain to begin their training. Two of this group W. Steele (standing, extreme left) and R. Coons (standing, extreme right) were killed when the R38 crashed on the 24 August 1921. (courtesy of the Navy Historical Centre, Washington)

The wreckage of the R38 after it had broken up over the River Humber, exploded and crashed into the river. The tail is on the left. (courtesy of the Navy Historical Centre, Washington)

The famous R100 airship built at Howden between 1926 and 1929. After the crash of the R101 airship over France, Britain's airship programme was abandoned and the R100 was scrapped.

Despite the inherent dangers of airships filled with hydrogen gas the R38 disaster of 1921 was not the end of the airship story in East Yorkshire. In 1924 the now derelict Howden airship station was reopened by the Airship Guarantee Co. (a division of Vickers Ltd) to build a new passenger-carrying airship, the R100. This was to be 709ft in length and be powered by six Rolls-Royce engines. In charge of the designers was Barnes Wallis (famous during the Second World War for his 'bouncing' bomb) while another member of the team was Neville Shute (later a famous novelist). Between 1926 and 1929 the R100 took shape in the large shed at Howden employing many local people, 60 per cent of them women employed, for example, in the fabric shop. The maiden flight of the giant airship took place at Howden on 16 December 1929 with the roads around congested with coaches bringing army personnel from Beverley, Pontefract and York to provide the ground-handling teams for manoeuvring the ship into position for take off. The maiden flight around York was a huge success and the R100 then set off for Cardington (Bedfordshire) where there was a mooring mast and which was earmarked as the airship's home base.

The main attraction of airships, compared to passenger carrying aircraft of the period, was the space and luxury that they could provide. The coach-mounted inside the hull of the R100 had three floors: two for the passengers and one for the crew. There were two and four-berth cabins and the opulent facilities were akin to travel by ocean-going liner. Yet despite a successful maiden flight to Canada the R100 was to fall victim to yet another airship disaster – that of its sister ship the R101. Built at the same time as the R100 the maiden flight of the R101 took place in October 1930 but ended in tragedy. Due to fly to India the airship ran into a storm over Northern France and crashed killing forty-eight of the people on board including the secretary of air, Lord Thompson. After this latest disaster confidence in airships as a form of travel quickly evaporated and the building programme was scrapped along with the successful Howden-built airship the R100.

Thus ended East Yorkshire's association with a form of transport that had seemed to promise much during the First World War but was ultimately to end in two major tragedies: that of the R38 over the River Humber and the R101 over France. With the end of airship production in Britain came the end of the airship station at Howden and these days few traces remain of a place that was once at the cutting-edge of aviation development.

19

Walkington's last Victorian Hayride

The East Riding village of Walkington was, until 2007, famous throughout the county for its annual Victorian Hayride (the inspiration of long-time Walkington resident, Ernie Teal). With a procession of horse-drawn vehicles, penny-fathing bicycles and village folk dressed in the clothes of bygone times, the Hayride became one of East Yorkshire's most cherished institutions, raising over £300,000 for charity in its forty-year history.

At first sight the village of Walkington, about two miles from the market town of Beverley, might appear little different from a host of other places in East Yorkshire. Situated in a dry valley with an east-west line its main street contains a mix of quaint cottages, modern houses, a village shop, three public houses and a picturesque duck pond. Sitting astride the B1230 road from Beverley to North Cave (and the M62 motorway) the village has been 'traffic calmed' in recent years.

However, what made Walkington distinctive from many other East Yorkshire villages was its thriving sense of community; it had long been an active village with the annual Victorian Hayride providing a major stimulus to village life. Alan Hardy moved to the village from Buckinghamshire some thirteen years with his wife Pam and two small children and from 1999 produced an online version of the popular *Walkington Newsletter*. As Alan said: 'Though the Hayride only took place over a weekend in June there was an undercurrent that ran through the entire year leading up to the big day when we all walked the route shaking our collection tins in aid of charity.'

The inspiration for the Hayride drew on the East Riding's rich agrarian past for one of the important dates in the farming calendar was a June holiday to mark the end of haymaking. Back in 1966 famous Walkington resident Ernie Teal, in search of a charity fundraising idea, recalled childhood stories of Victorian times when people would dress up in their best clothes and travel by horse-drawn wagons to the seaside. The following year his nostalgic idea bore fruit when the first horses and wagons left Northlands Farm on the first of Walkington's 'new-look' hayrides.

The Walkington Hayrides of 1967-2007 were in fact an apt reminder of Walkington's own past for long before it was a dormitory settlement for Beverley and Hull the village was a farming community. In the early nineteenth century when the population of Walkington was about 300 people a local directory listed twenty-one farmers in the village. There were also a host of other trades both to support farming and a rural community at a time when limited transport meant the village had to be far more self-sufficient than it is today. Back in 1823 Walkington had four shoemakers and two tailors together with other tradesmen like carpenters and blacksmiths.

The red-hot fire of the blacksmith's forge and the sound of his hammer on the anvil would once have been familiar sights and sounds behind the Ferguson-Fawsitt Arms in the village where generations of these craftsmen shoed horses and repaired farm implements. The last of these, Thomas Bailey, worked in the village for almost forty years before, in 1950, his blacksmith's shop became the cocktail bar of the Ferguson-Fawsitt Arms.

The name of this public house is, in fact, an important reminder of the landed family who once held sway here. Daniel Ferguson had arrived in Walkington in 1808 as rector of All Hallows' church

The village pond at the East End of Walkington was formed in a natural hollow.

and ten years later had begun much needed restoration work on the building. One of his thirteen children, Major John Daniel Ferguson, married, in 1866, the heiress Anne Fawsitt from a rich local landowning family and together the Ferguson-Fawsitt's lived at Walkington Hall. After the death of the major in 1908 the estate passed to Gertrude and Henry Chater Fawsitt. In a way the strong social conscience of Walkington folk today can be traced back to this couple for the Fawsitts were important local benefactors. Mrs Fawsitt provided a reading room in the village together with newspapers and, since the village school in Northgate (opened in 1876) had no playing field, the Fawsitts gave the headmaster recreational use of the deer paddock on the eastern side of Walkington Hall. The couple died in 1933 within two months of each other. However, in a real sense the Ferguson-Fawsitts have left their mark on the Walkington of today not only with the name of the public house but also with their landscaping, wall building and tree planting.

Another philanthropist who was active in Walkington in the early twentieth century was the Hull industrialist Sir James Reckitt. In 1917 he bought a house and land in order to establish the Hull Aftercare Colony, a facility for the victims of tuberculosis, when, in the days before antibiotics, fresh air and exercise were considered to be important in helping TB victims to recover. After the Second World War the Aftercare Colony became the Walkington Riding Stables.

Although the village of Walkington has existed for over a millennium (it was referred to in the eleventh-century Domesday Book as Walchinton), the most dramatic changes have only happened in the last sixty years. The rise of private motoring since the Second World War has helped to make

All Hallows' church, Walkington, stands on the southern shoulder of Walkington's dry valley and dates from at least AD 1100. In 1808 Daniel Ferguson arrived as rector of Walkington and the effective owner of one-sixth of the parish.

Walkington a very desirable place to live and by 1981 new housing developments, like those off Saunders Lane, had helped to swell the population to over 1,800 people. In the 1990s there was further house building at the eastern extremity of the village when the old Broadgate Hospital was demolished.

To compensate the villagers for their loss of the sports hall at the hospital the developers paid the village £250,000 for the building of a new village hall (opened in 1993). Both the Hayride and the village hall helped to foster Walkington's unique appeal. As Ernie Teal, who had spent most of his eighty-seven years in the village (and was awarded an MBE for his services to the community), put it: 'Walkington has always been an active village with a strong sense of community.'

In Ernie's opinion the heyday of the Walkington Hayride was in the 1970s when everyone in the village was involved in the spectacle and with some even making their own costumes for the big day. Why then, after forty years, did the Hayride to come to an end? Ernie Teal suggested that the main reasons were: 'The difficulties of finding enough heavy shire horses to pull the wagons and the modern-day health and safety issues involved in organising such a huge event.'

Others, like Alan Hardy, had another explanation: 'It was becoming more difficult getting the crowds out as years went by and it was probably better to bring it to a conclusion rather than letting it peter out.'

The men leading the final parade on Sunday 17 June 2007 were Geoff Morton and his son Mark, who still use horses on their farm near Holme on Spalding Moor. Their shire horses and wagon had

Above left: Hayride Garden Party. (courtesy of Alan Hardy of Walkington)

Above right: Heavy horses pull the Hayride wagons. (courtesy of Alan Hardy of Walkington)

also taken part in the first Walkington Victorian Hayride in 1967 when Mark was only seven! As before, the procession of decorated horse-drawn vehicles set off from the village to cover the eleven-mile circular route via Bishop Burton, the Westwood, and Beverley.

However, the end of the Hayride has not meant the end of fundraising efforts or indeed of Walkington's indomitable community spirit for two attractions associated with the event, a barn dance and a garden party have continued as before.

A look at the *Walkington Newsletter* of recent years reveal that there has been much more to the village than just the Hayride: an annual Christmas Fayre, a pantomime, monthly quiz nights, beetle drives and a 'Cub Scout' group were just some of the social activities on offer. As relative newcomers to the village Paul and Jo Acklam (of the Beverley firm of Acklam's Coaches) enthused: 'There have been many stimulating activities in Walkington and most age groups have been catered for.'

For such a dynamic community the end of the Hayride in June 2007 (although sad) is unlikely to hinder Walkington's impressive sense of community in the long term.

20

When Mother Nature Wrought Havoc

The subject of the weather has long been regarded as a peculiarly British obsession, partly because of the unpredictability of the United Kingdom's maritime climate. In late June 2007, however, concerns about climate change took on a whole new significance with the most disastrous floods that Yorkshire has ever seen. Yet as the history books show the county is no stranger to the wrath of 'Mother Nature'…

The East Riding of Yorkshire is often seen as one of the drier, sheltered, parts of the British Isles since for much of the time the prevailing winds are from the southwest. However, from time to time, East Yorkshire too has been on the receiving end of the kind of extreme weather conditions experienced elsewhere. On the 25 June 2007 the city of Hull and parts of the East Riding were visited by the greatest catastrophe to afflict the area in modern times: flooding on a huge scale. Following over twenty-four hours of torrential rain that had begun to fall on Sunday 24 June, Hull's drains could no longer cope with the sheer volume of water and streets were turned into raging torrents. 95 per cent of the city is below sea level and there was simply nowhere for the water to go. According to meteorologists Hull received a sixth of its annual rainfall in just twelve hours of intense downpours and the results for the city were disastrous. Large areas of Hull, like Kingswood, Corona Drive, Newland Avenue, Priory Road and Norland Avenue, were turned into lakes and the water soon began to flood into homes and business premises too. By 3 p.m. on Monday 25 June the Great Yorkshire Flood had claimed its first victim: a twenty-eight-year-old man become trapped when trying to clear a drain in West Hull. He died of hypothermia despite valiant attempts to rescue him. Meanwhile the emergency services were overwhelmed with calls from desperate householders across the city whose homes were beginning to fill with water and sewage.

The immense scale and cost of this humanitarian disaster was soon apparent for 10,500 houses had to be evacuated and it was estimated that over 16,000 homes had been affected in some way (about one in ten of the city's households). Although the floods devastated other part of Yorkshire too, like Sheffield and Doncaster, the Environment Agency said that Hull was the worst affected with damage to public property alone put at over £200 million. In some quarters the neglect of Hull's system of drainage dikes and sewers was highlighted as a cause of the disaster while in others the failure of emergency pumping equipment was blamed.

Other parts of the East Riding too bore the brunt of the unseasonal June weather with villages like Burstwick, Hedon, Skilaugh and Leven suffering flooded streets and houses. In the East Riding 2,000 homes were affected by floodwater. Here too failings in flood preparation and maintenance became apparent: the outlet at Hedon Haven was built to carry pumps but these had never been installed.

In Beverley properties closest to the historic Westwood Pasture, like Willow Grove, suffered a repeat of the disastrous floods of almost a century earlier. On 27 July 1912 a local newspaper reported a 'cloud burst' over Beverley and Cottingham with 1.86in rain falling in ninety minutes. Houses in Willow Grove were soon 1ft deep in water and as their inhabitants retreated to the upper floors the Market Place in the centre of town took on the appearance of a lake.

Chanterlands Avenue, Hull on the late afternoon of Monday 25 June 2007. The initial euphoria of watching someone surf on flooded streets soon gave way to despair, as homes were flooded. (courtesy of Les Fisher)

At the Tiger Inn in Lairgate the landlord, Joe Brown, reported that his barrels were 'swimming about in the cellar' while at Well Place (off Well Lane) one of Beverley's poorer inhabitants complained:

> *I had two feet of water in the house. The fire had been completely put out by the water. My bread had been washed out of the cupboard and was floating about the room. I have been married for eighteen years and had eleven bairns but never had ought like this in my life before.*

The *Beverley Guardian* of 27 July 1912 reported that at the junction of Walkergate, Toll Gavel and Butcher Row the water was 18in deep and 'some twenty or thirty children were quickly disporting themselves in it having divested themselves of their shoes and stockings'.

Compared to June 2007 however the rainfall that caused the Beverley floods of 1912 was both more localized and of shorter duration. A local newspaper records that at Hull Bridge, about two miles east of Beverley, only 0.15in of rain fell while at the East Riding Asylum near Walkington it was 2.5in. During the downpours of June 2007 affecting the whole East Riding, about 4in of rain fell.

One of the East Riding villages scarred by the inundations of long ago was Langtoft, a settlement high in the Yorkshire Wolds north of Driffield. A plaque in the centre of the village records the 'Great Flood of Langtoft' in both 1657 and 1892. The local media of the time reported that:

> *On the Sunday evening July 3rd 1892 there was a most destructive cloud burst when the rush of water completely washed away three or four cottages and did an immense amount of damage to the property of the villagers, who are of the poorer class.*

Eighteen years later it was the turn of Driffield to experience the wrath of nature. Throughout history the appearance of a comet has often been seen as an omen of ill-fortune. On 19 May 1910 the Earth passed through the tail of a regular visitor to the solar system: Hailey's Comet. On the following day, Friday 20 May, Driffield was 'visited' by one of the greatest calamities ever to have afflicted the tow: the Great Flood of 1910. Whether the passage of Hailey's Comet was a coincidence or a portent of doom is, of course, open to argument. What was soon apparent to Driffield residents were the results of the freak weather of that day.

The Beverley Guardian of 27 July 1912 reported that at the junction of Walkergate, Toll Gavel and Butcher Row the water was 18in deep and 'some twenty or thirty children were quickly disporting themselves in it having divested themselves of their shoes and stockings.'

The village of Langtoft north of Driffield lies at the bottom of a dale and is famous for its freak weather conditions in days gone by.

The 'Great Storm' began at 4 a.m. with peals of thunder and vivid flashes of lightening which were soon followed by ferocious hail and rain. Accounts from the time show that as hailstones 1.5in in diameter fell and streets became rivers there was panic as householders tried to make their properties safe from the inrush of water.

Worse was soon to follow: by 5.30 a.m. word arrived that a torrent of water was fast approaching the town from the Wolds. By 7 a.m. Driffield was inundated by an inrush of water and mud that flooded the streets between Middle Street and Eastgate, the cattle market and the Driffield gas works. Since the deluge quickly extinguished the furnaces there an appeal went out to householders to conserve supplies as 'no more gas could be made for some time.'

Even after the water had subsided Driffield had to cope with the aftermath since thousands of tons of mud had been swept into the streets and houses. Although there was only one fatality, 150 houses had to be cleared of debris that, in some cases, was 2ft deep. To help with the distress caused a fund relief committee was established to appeal for funds and this raised over £800, a considerable sum by early twentieth-century standards.

Over on the coast at Bridlington the most serious weather disaster was the 'Great Gale' of 1871. On 8 February a fleet of about 400 vessels had set sail from the River Tyne heading south but had become becalmed in Bridlington Bay. At around 2 a.m. on 10 February a violent southeasterly gale blew up and accompanied by sleet and snow threatened to drive ashore the ships at anchor. Horrified onlookers at Bridlington Harbour watched the drama unfold.

Mountainous seas and limited resources made the task of would-be rescuers almost impossible and seventeen ships were forced onto the shoreline where they were broken up by the pounding waves. Bridlington had two lifeboats powered by oars: the *Robert Whitworth* and the *Harbinger* and they were soon at work to save as many of the crews as they could. Tragically the *Harbinger* capsized during a daring attempt to rescue the captain of a Whitby-owned brig who was clinging to the stern of his ship, the *Delta*. Both he and six members of the crew of the *Harbinger* were drowned in the tragedy.

If it had not been for the heroic efforts of the two lifeboats many more lives would have been lost that day. As it was Bridlington's 'Great Gale' of February 1871 led to around seventy deaths and the loss of thirty ships. Twenty-three victims of the disaster were buried during a mass funeral at Bridlington's priory church on 14 February with the funeral procession through the town being watched by an estimated 4,000 onlookers.

While storms may bring, in the words of the hymn, 'peril on the sea', severe winter weather usually means travel disruption of all kinds for those on land. The intense winter of February and March 1947 was made worse by post-war shortages of coal and other materials and this added to the general feeling of gloom. Reports in local newspapers of the time (reduced to a war-time size of four pages to save paper) give an indication of the struggle to keep open roads blocked by snow. On 10 February 1947, for example, the chairman of Beverley Town Council was asked to explain the state of the main route out of the town along Eastgate, Flemingate and Beckside since it had been 'in a most treacherous condition'. Twelve days later the *Yorkshire Post* reported that roads already cleared once were blocked again and that 'by midnight the snowfall over a large part of Yorkshire had lasted for more than twenty-four hours.' In East Yorkshire two passenger trains became stuck in drifts while council workmen trying to clear roads blocked by snow were withdrawn when the job became impossible (22 February 1947).

Worst hit were the farms and villages of the higher ground of the Yorkshire Wolds, swept by blizzards and drifting snow and where, in the words of the *Driffield Times* on 8 March 1947: 'One of the worst storms in half a century is still dislocating transport and has caused serious losses among sheep flocks.'

The same newspaper reported on the struggles of the postmaster of Thwing on a journey to Wold Newton, two miles away. He made the trip on horseback since the deep snow made it impossible for him to travel on foot but when, at journey's end, the horse broke free he was left stranded!

Extremes of weather have therefore been a factor in the history of East Yorkshire for centuries although in many cases the problems they created were more localized. There is little doubt that the unprecedented flooding that took place in Hull and the East Riding in June 2007 was more severe than anything people had experienced before and given the scale of the devastation will take much longer to put right.

21

James Reckitt and Swanland

One of the most remarkable features about Swanland (seven miles to the west of Hull) is its rapid growth in recent times for although it retains a village atmosphere it has taken on the dimensions of a small town. At the beginning of the twentieth century it was like most other East Yorkshire villages: a self-sufficient community dominated by the needs of farming and with a population numbering 463. It was to this peaceful rural community that the powerful industrialist James Reckitt came in 1884 and took up residence at Swanland Manor…

The charms of modern-day Swanland, most evident around its beautiful village pond and a number of listed buildings along its main street and West End, were not lost on earlier visitors to the village. A directory of 1823 pointed to the breathtaking views available from this ancient hilltop settlement:

The landscapes seen from this village are greatly admired by visitors for their beauty, variety and grandeur. An elevated spot near Swanland Mill commands a view of the Trent and the country adjacent together with the whole course of the Humber down to Spurn lights.

Yet the number of houses in the village did not increase significantly in the nineteenth century partly because, one suspects, any new inhabitants wishing to work elsewhere would have faced a two mile uphill walk from the nearest railway station at North Ferriby!

One important new arrival however was the Quaker industrialist James Reckitt who moved here from Hessle and took up residence in the summer of 1884 at Swanland Manor House. From his correspondence it becomes clear that Reckitt considered Swanland to be a very desirable place to live since he was surrounded by 'lovely gardens and fine scenery' and he continued to have an important influence on the village as a JP and a benefactor until his death in 1924.

James Reckitt had been born at Nottingham in 1833, the son of Isaac Reckitt a miller and corn dealer. In 1840 Isaac Reckitt had bought a starch business in Hull and James began working for him eight years later as a travelling salesman. This family firm prospered with starch, laundry blue and black lead being manufactured in the factory off Dansom Lane. When Isaac Reckitt died in 1862, James and two of his brothers carried on the business as a partnership. Through advertising, the creation of brand names and clever marketing the name of Reckitt became an international success story in the manufacture of household products. By 1914 Reckitt & Sons Ltd was a multinational manufacturing company with an expanding range of products like Zebra and Brasso and employing more than 5,000 people.

By the late nineteenth century James Reckitt was already a wealthy man active in both business and politics (as chairman of the local Liberal Association) and in 1894 he accepted a knighthood. A firm believer in the doctrine of self-improvement he was quite prepared to pour his own money into ventures he believed would benefit the wider community. One of these was the provision of free libraries and to set an example to the rest of Hull he donated the James Reckitt Library in Holderness Road (1889) with a stock of over 8,000 books.

Above left: The Hull industrialist Sir James Reckitt lived at Swanland Manor for forty years from 1884-1924. The Reckitt family made numerous gifts to the village including the land on which the tennis courts and the bowling green stand. (courtesy of Reckitt Benckiser, Hull)

Above right: In the days before detergents products like Reckitt's Laundry Blue were added to the final rinse to make clothes look whiter than white. It was manufactured household goods like these that created growing prosperity for the company and wealth for the Reckitt family.

One of the most lasting legacies of his charitable instincts was the creation of a 'garden village' in East Hull. Motivated by the squalid living conditions that many of Hull's working-class people had to endure at the beginning of the twentieth century and inspired by 'model villages' built elsewhere in Britain by philanthropists like the Cadbury Bros at Bourneville, near Birmingham, he made a start in 1907. He bought a 130-acre site from the Jalland family off Holderness Road in Hull in order to bring the kind of country living he enjoyed in Swanland to his employees in Hull. His aim was to provide good-quality houses with gardens for the same rent as the city centre slums endured by working-class families. The houses had running water, decent sanitation, gas lighting, plenty of windows to let in light while the whole of his 'Garden Village' project was designed to promote a rustic feel. There was even a village green (the Oval), a village hall and a library.

The philanthropy of the Reckitt family towards Swanland itself was legendary too for Sir James saw it as his Christian duty to help those less fortunate than himself. At Christmas there was a huge distribution of Christmas boxes with gifts of blankets, ham, bread and money to needy villagers while he was also active in supporting the local school (e.g. by providing prizes for good attendance) and by supplying 1,500 books as the nucleus for a village library. One of his lasting legacies was the Institute, opened in 1914 and built to house two billiard rooms and a reading room/library for the self-improvement of Swanlanders. Another of the Reckitt bequests to the village, the Swanland Memorial Hall (built in memory of Sir James by his son), is now part of the Swanland Primary School

On 14 July Sir Philip Reckitt attended a meeting of Swanland Parish Council to state that he wished to build a hall in memory of his father, Sir James Reckitt. The Swanland Memorial Hall is now part of Swanland Primary School.

on Tranby Lane while donations of land allowed for the creation of a bowling green and tennis courts which are still very much a part of the Swanland of today.

Basil Reckitt writing in 1981 described Sir James as the 'father figure' of Swanland even though another important family the Todds (who lived at Swanland Hall) were benefactors before him. It was John Todd who paid for a new school building at Swanland (opened in 1876) and an extension to it in later years. Part of the old school now serves as the village hall.

Despite the presence of another powerful local family there is no denying that the strict morality of Sir James Reckitt continued to exert a considerable influence on Swanland for the forty years he lived there and even in the decades after his death. When Swanland Parish Council was established in 1894 Sir James Reckitt was elected as its chairman while his interest in improving the lot of ordinary villagers was shown by his donation of land for a waterworks at around the same time. Local business and employment also benefited from his presence at Swanland Manor with a village tailor providing the livery for his servants. He even provided a street lamp on the Village Institute building supplied by the electric generator at Swanland Manor in the days before the village had mains electricity.

Yet although he was generous to the village his strict code of morality exerted a powerful controlling influence too. His high-mindedness can be seen in the rules of the institute he created when it was stated that the aim was one of 'moral and intellectual improvement' while another rule stated that there was to be no form of gambling on the premises. This same morality can be seen in his attitude to alcohol. After the local public house, the White Horse, lost its licence over an alcohol-related death

The Swanland Institute was paid for by Sir James Reckitt and opened in 1914. He even provided a street lamp on the building supplied by the electric generator at Swanland Manor in the days before the village had mains electricity.

the Reckitt prejudice against 'demon-drink' helped to ensure that Swanland remained a 'dry' village for over eighty years. The modern-day village pub (the Swan and Cygnet) only opened its doors for the first time in 1980.

While he was able to exert his considerable influence against alcohol in a small community like Swanland it was more difficult in Hull where there many public houses close to the factory in Dansom Lane to tempt his workforce. However, he did ensure that there was no public house in his 'Garden Village' project and told its residents that he hoped that they would cut their average weekly spending on alcohol from 7s to 3s.

In a sense the contemporary growth of Swanland since the Second World War owes much to the Todds and the Reckitts since much of the land used to build its post-war housing developments was freed by the demolition of Swanland Manor and Swanland Hall. In 1926 the Todd estate was sold at auction and its land bordering Tranby Lane was, for example, disposed of as building plots at the bargain price (in today's terms) of around £185 each! Similarly, the demolition of Swanland Manor in 1935 made other land available for housing development. Schemes like those in Northfield in the 1970s and the sheltered-housing scheme at Haldenby Court in the 1990s have meant that Swanland remains an attractive proposition both for those with growing families and for the retired.

22

Pioneering Aviation at Hedon Aerodrome

The growth of air travel in the last sixty years has seen the development of regional airports throughout the United Kingdom. Today's local passengers have a choice of Humberside, Doncaster, Leeds-Bradford, East Midlands and Manchester Airports all within two hours travelling distance of East Yorkshire. Back in the 1930s, however, air services were even closer. Hedon Aerodrome, on the eastern side of Hull, bore witness to some of the earliest pioneering efforts in aviation…

By the early twentieth century municipal enterprise was already a feature of the growth of Hull with the Corporation providing everyday public services like water, gas and electricity to its citizens. In 1895 Hull Corporation had also bought Hull's developing tramway system and in 1904 it established a municipal telephone service that ten years later became the sole provider in the Hull area. Against this background therefore the decision to establish a municipal airport was not unusual especially since other important cities, like Manchester, had already taken steps to embrace this new form of travel. Civic pride meant that Hull could not be left behind in the race. From September 1928, the Hull Chamber of Commerce had been campaigning to establish an air service between Hull and the Continent for the transport of mail. The following year the Air Ministry gave the Corporation permission to acquire land at Hedon Racecourse for a municipal aerodrome and for it to begin operations 'as soon as the levelling operations and other work was completed.' (July 1929). When all was ready Hull's lord mayor made the trip to London to collect the Air Ministry licences marking approval for the opening of Hull's new municipal airport (7 October 1929).

The racecourse at Twyers Farm had, because of dwindling popularity, ceased to operate twenty years earlier but the course with its one-mile straight was suitable for pioneering aircraft to take off and land. The first British powered flight in a heavier-than-air machine had taken place in October 1908 but this aeroplane had only been airborne for twenty-seven seconds! Early encouragement for aviation was provided by the *Daily Mail* and the national newspaper gave publicity to many pioneering efforts. In 1912 the paper told its readers that a young German, Gustav Hamel, would be arriving in Hull for the first flight to take place over the city. In the event Hamel arrived by train with his Bleriot monoplane in a packing case ready to be assembled!

The first flight at the old Hedon Racecourse, on the afternoon of 13 July 1912, attracted a large excited crowd eager to watch Mr Hamel's efforts. As the *Daily Mail* reported:

The crowd was filled with doubts as to whether the airman would clear the rails in the distance but this fear was soon removed for he quickly reached a height of about 500 feet and sailed away amidst a storm of applause.

Hamel's second flight lasted thirty-two minutes took him over Hull, Hedon, Preston and Sutton before he returned to the racecourse. His third flight, following the railway line, towards Withernsea ended prematurely when he ran into a bank of low cloud two miles from the sea and decided to return.

Hedon Racecourse operated between 1888-1909 on the site of Twyers Farm. After the closure of the racecourse it was used for the pioneering flights of Gustav Hamel in July 1912.

With the development of better aircraft during the First World War and the 1920s came the need for organised aerodromes even if these only had grass runways. The purchase, for £17,400, of the 200-acre site at Hedon for Hull's Municipal Airport in 1929 was in fact only part of much grander plans. The minutes of the aerodrome committee show that there were also moves afoot to lease four acres of land and a pier at Paull (a nearby village on the Humber) for transporting passengers from land aeroplanes to seaplanes. To encourage the use of the aerodrome, part of the site was also leased to National Flying Services Ltd for the Hull Aero Club to build a hangar and for a bungalow as an office and clubhouse. Negotiations were also underway, by 1930, with the Civilian Aircraft Co. of Burton-on-Trent to lease land at the aerodrome for a small aircraft factory.

The estimated 40,000 people who turned up for the official opening of the new aerodrome 10 October 1929) indicated the public's fascination with air travel. After the opening ceremony carried out HRH Prince George of Kent came an air pageant with receipts of over £1,400. Enthusiastic aerodrome crowds were also a feature of the homecoming of Hull's favourite daughter of the inter-war years: Amy Johnson.

Amy Johnson had been born in Hull in 1903 and after university had moved to London in search of work. Fascinated by the images of flying she had seen at the cinema she joined the London Flying Club in 1928 and a year later gained her full pilot's licence. Amy now decided to prove herself as an aviator with the kind of record-breaking flight so much in vogue in the 1920s. Her goal was to fly from England to Australia and beat the record of fifteen days established in 1928. Supported by the oil tycoon Lord Wakefield, Amy bought a two-year-old Gipsy Moth biplane with an open cockpit and a 9m wingspan and gave it the name of *Jason*. After she left on 5 May 1930 the story of a young woman flying solo to Australia captured the public imagination and by the time she reached Darwin on the 24 May she was well on the way to being a celebrity. Though Amy Johnson did not break the record that she had cherished, the publicity generated by the *Daily Mail* (who bought her story for £10,000) helped to ensure her immortality in the annals of aviation.

On 11 August 1930, escorted by nine other planes, Amy flew *Jason* into Hedon Aerodrome to the kind of rapturous welcome reserved for national heroes with the Hull Police Band playing *Hail the Conquering Hero Comes* and the crowd cheering and waving flags. The lord mayor then gave a speech in honour of 'Hull's most distinguished woman citizen' before the official party retired inside the clubhouse for afternoon tea, further speeches and a presentation of a diamond brooch to the guest of honour. This was but the start of a day of celebration for soon after a motorcade left the aerodrome for a ten-mile journey through the streets of Hull, the route lined with crowds of cheering people, a reception at the City Hall and an evening banquet in Amy's honour at the Guildhall.

During her speech to this distinguished audience of civic leaders Hull's aviation heroine pointed out, with her usual northern bluntness, that although 'Hull had a fine aerodrome she had not found a large number of machines going up. At one place in Australia she was told that forty women had joined the local aero club'.

Perhaps stung by her criticism the Aerodrome Committee held talks with National Flying Services, in January 1931, on ways to attract more people to the aerodrome and there were even suggestions of building tennis courts, croquet lawns and a golf course! With flying still in its infancy there was still much to be gained from publicity, although plans for another air pageant (on the 7 June 1931)

After her famous flight to Australia (5-24 May 1930) Amy Johnson flew into Hedon Aerodrome on the 11 August 1930 to a hero's welcome.

An air pageant in the early 1930s. In the background, fronting Hedon Road is the Airport Garage (formerly the aircraft factory of the Civilian Aircraft Company before it went into liquidation in 1933). (courtesy of Hedon Museum)

met with strong criticism from Hull's Wesleyan Methodists because the event was to be held on a Sunday!

Yet despite air pageants and well-publicised open days with free admission (like the one held by Hull Aero Club on May 1934 to foster public interest in aviation), progress was slow. More significant for the reputation of the airport was the start of commercial services like that to Grimsby in July 1933. This 'Humber Air Ferry', using a twin-engined Blackburn Segrave, was however only a short-lived venture. Another highlight of Hedon's schedule in the thirties was a Liverpool-Hedon-Amsterdam service each week operated by the international airline KLM (beginning in June 1934). This Dutch airline had built up a reputation in the 1920s and early 1930s for the standard of its service and a Daimler saloon was provided to take passengers from the Hull's Royal Station Hotel to the municipal airport. Here they would climb aboard a KLM Fokker FX11 aircraft equipped with three engines and sixteen passenger seats.

However, the aerodrome was not without its critics and as early as October 1930 it emerged that the firm of British Industrial Solvents had been complaining to the Air Ministry in London about low flying over their factory at Salt End. In March 1935 one Hull councillor, G.K. Spruit, went so far as to say that Hedon was unsuitable for an aerodrome and with Salt End's oil tanks close by it is easy to understand his reasoning on safety grounds alone. By 1939 Hull Corporation were considering plans for a new aerodrome at the safer location of Neatmarsh Road, Preston but these schemes came to nothing for in the same month that work was due to start, September 1939, the Second World War began.

This put paid not only to Hull's new airport plans but also to the existing municipal airport at

The most significant of Hedon's commercial flights was the weekly KLM service to Amsterdam that began in June 1934. Shown here are the passengers and crew in front of a KLM Fokker FX 11 aircraft. (courtesy of Hedon Museum)

Hedon. In 1939 the Air Ministry requisitioned the aerodrome and to prevent its possible use as a landing ground during a German invasion hundreds of old cars were abandoned there. An anti-aircraft battery was also established to fire at German bombers attacking Hull.

In 1943 Hull Corporation sought powers to re-establish the airport once hostilities were over, but nothing became of these plans or those in the 1960s (supported by the firm of Priestmans) to establish a service from the old aerodrome to London. Instead the wartime RAF airfield at Kirmington, south of the river, was developed as Humberside Airport in the 1970s. Ironically the first scheduled flight out of Humberside, in 1975, was to Amsterdam – the same international destination served by Hedon in the 1930s!

Anyone driving from the direction of Salt End roundabout into Hedon today and looking at the rough grazing land on their left will search in vain for signs of an airport. Yet it was here in the 1930s that history was made at Hedon Aerodrome with the triumphant return of Amy Johnson after her epic flight to Australia and the launch of commercial air services in East Yorkshire.

23

Of Unsound Mind

Although the subject of mental ill-health is often seen by many as a taboo subject the fact remains that one in four people will, at some point in their lives, suffer a mental health problem. The mother with post-natal depression, a young woman with eating disorders, the disruptive school pupil with behavioural problems, the elderly patient ravaged by Alzheimer's disease or the victim of a car accident suffering from post-traumatic stress disorder are only a few examples of those who suffer mental ill-health. While in the twenty-first century 'Community Care' is the preferred option of helping the mentally ill, the systems and methods used in the past were far different. In earlier times institutional care in either private or public asylums was often the preferred option…

Like so many other aspects of medicine, progress in treating those with mental health problems remained painfully slow until recent times. Doctors in the eighteenth and nineteenth centuries might use crude devices like the swivel chair to treat mental illness. This was used to spin a depressed patient at high speed in the forlorn hope that this would rearrange the content of his or her brain into the right position.

To calm those with manias baths were considered to have sedative properties, while cold showers were used to treat those with melancholia (depression). Although such methods may have distracted patients momentarily they did not offer any real relief.

The eighteenth and early nineteenth centuries saw the development of some private asylums in the East Riding to house people with mental-health problems. One of these was Moor Cottage near Brandesburton which operated between 1821 and 1851. Plans in the East Riding Archive in Beverley (dated 29 September 1828) show a large institution with separate day rooms for men and women, sleeping accommodation on the upper floors and airing courts for the patients (fresh air and exercise were seen as an important part of the treatment).

Reports from visiting magistrates who supervised the running of the asylum make fascinating reading with frequent references to the very excited state of the inmates, especially in hot weather! Since Moor Cottage was a private asylum and had been created to make money for its owners (the Beal Family), the care of the inmates had to be paid for, sometimes by reluctant parish authorities in the East Riding. In May 1836 the magistrates received representations from the Overseers of the Poor of Foston-on-the-Wolds asking for the discharge from the asylum of Jacob Ibotson. However, the magistrates declined to do so after listening to the views of a visiting surgeon who considered Ibotson to be 'a dangerous idiot and an improper person to be at liberty.' Yet, at a time when mental illness was not properly understood, it seems that Ibotson's incarceration at the Moor Cottage Ayslum was due only to epileptic fits.

During a visit in December 1850 the magistrates found that some of the female patients had not been out of doors for several weeks. Some patients could be troublesome and one of them tried to escape three times and had attempted to murder one of the attendants and set fire to the asylum.

Certificates of admission held by the East Riding Archive record the names of some patients. On 15 March 1829, for example, we learn of the confinement of Miss Elizabeth Johnson, a

Crude devices such as the 'spinning chair' were used to treat the mentally ill in the early nineteenth century.

Early nineteenth-century advertisement for the Moor Cottage Private Asylum at Brandesburton. It was claimed that the new establishment offered 'salubrity of the air, extensive grounds for exercise and the facility for sea-bathing being but a short distance from the coast'. The asylum was opened in 1821 by John Beal but when his son Joseph Beal applied to magistrates for a renewal of its thirty-year licence in September 1851 this was turned down.

Private Asylum,

MOOR COTTAGE,

Near Brands-Burton, Yorkshire;

Only 8 Miles from Beverley, 9 from Driffield, 12 from Bridlington Quay, 5 from Hornsea, 17 from Hull, and immediately adjoining the Road to Scarborough.

schoolmistress of Beverley. Her sisters had arranged her stay in the Moor Cottage Asylum with the agreement of two Beverley surgeons although we do not know why she was sent there. After a time she must have been released for on 6 September 1829 she was admitted for a second time.

The visiting magistrates were sometimes critical of what they found on their visits and on 6 November 1837 they reported that the rooms and premises generally were in a poor order and that 'many of the inmates appear in a very excited state'. During the same visit they suggested that a straw mattress be provided for Mrs Collins to stop her injuring herself 'in her present distressing condition'. The difficulties that the staff had with some patients was indicated by a recommendation of November 1850 that 'in the case of patients who have dirty habits we recommend that they should sleep upon clean straw covered with a sheet or a blanket that can be changed as necessary.'

John Beal had established the Moor Cottage Asylum in 1821 and when he retired in 1839 his son Joseph continued with the business. However, in 1846 there were only seven inmates and in September 1851 his application to magistrates for a renewal of his licence to run the asylum was refused.

Despite an obvious need to care for the mentally ill it was not until 1845 that state provision of lunatic asylums became compulsory. This led to the building of a joint asylum for North and East Yorkshire at Clifton, York in 1847. However, within twenty years the rising cost of this asylum, to East Riding taxpayers, led to plans for a separate institution. In 1865 advertisements appeared in local newspapers stating that land was needed to build a new East Riding Lunatic Asylum. After considering several possibilities (including sites at Malton, Bempton and Molescroft) the organising committee chose Broadgate Farm near Walkington. Work on the new asylum began in the spring of 1869 and it received its first intake of patients in October 1871. The hospital complex covered 13,500 square yards of land and included two airing courts for the recreational use of male and female patients. In the days before electricity the buildings were lit by gas provided by the asylum's own gas works.

By the beginning of 1872 there were 195 patients at the East Riding Lunatic Asylum and, according to a report of the medical superintendent, Dr Mercer, attempts at escape had been 'few and abortive'. As a part of the asylum's regime attention was given to recreational activities and to this end he recorded that a picnic excursion to Westella had been organised for twenty women patients as well as weekly balls and occasional concerts at the asylum itself. To ensure that the patients benefited from the 'wondrous moral hygiene of industry' those who were capable of working found employment in the asylum's gardens, and its joinery, shoemaking, tailoring, bricklaying and blacksmith workshops.

The East Riding Lunatic Asylum opened in Walkington in October 1871 (renamed the East Riding Mental Hospital in November 1920). (courtesy of Beverley Local Studies Library)

The Walkington asylum was subject to the usual checks on its operations by inspectors and other visitors. A visit in January 1874, for example, reported that 160 inmates had sat down to a dinner of boiled bacon, greens, bread and beer and that this 'seemed to give satisfaction to all and that the conduct of the patients was most orderly'. Yet, from other evidence, it is apparent that the asylum staff faced danger from some of the inmates as Dr Mercer pointed out in a report of January 1876. He referred to an assault on the asylum's matron, Mary Harrison, by a 'dangerous and athletic female lunatic' who had all her life been of 'ungovernable temper'. Mercer commented that this was a striking example of the risks taken by those 'who earn their daily bread in a daily intercourse with the insane.'

A report of December 1878 records, in graphic detail, the trauma (for the staff) of keeping watch on potential suicide cases. A female patient having failed in two previous suicide attempts tried again, during dinner, by pushing a meat bone into her larynx. Medical staff then had to make an opening in her trachea in order to remove it. Even after this the staff had to make use of restraints to stop the unfortunate woman from tearing open her throat wound. In the words of the medical superintendent this kind of episode added enormously to the 'anxious and arduous responsibilities of asylum officers' and perhaps helps to explain the high turnover of staff. A report of 1881 said that of the ten nurses employed at the asylum, five had not yet completed one year's service while of ten male attendants six were in the same position. The lunacy commissioners who compiled the report lamented the frequent changes of staff and said these were detrimental to patient welfare.

The 1881 census, while not revealing the names of individual patients, does show us that the inmates came from a wide cross-section of society; the former occupations of asylum residents ranged from a dentist to dressmakers and farm labourers. The East Riding Lunatic Asylum (renamed the East Riding Mental Hospital in November 1920) benefited from general progress in understanding the causes of mental illness. Research into both the biological and psychological aspects of mental illness led to new theories and treatments. Prominent among researchers into the psychological causes was Sigmund Freud (1856-1939) who argued that the source of mental illness lay in unconscious conflicts originating in early childhood experiences. The search for organic causes of mental health problems led to new remedies involving sedatives (like morphine) and the development of deep-sleep treatment. More controversial was the use (from 1938) of electro-convulsive therapy as a treatment for severe depression and in some cases of schizophrenia and mania. Electro-convulsive therapy (used at both the Broadgate Hospital and at the De la Pole Hospital in Willerby) involved placing electrodes on the temples, on one or both sides of the patient's head, and delivering a small electric current.

In 1946 the National Health Act was passed and Broadgate Mental Hospital (as it became known) ceased to be independent and was now a component part of the NHS. During the 1950s the tradition of caring for mentally ill people in large institutions came under intense criticism while in the 1960s the development of new drugs meant that it was now possible to treat patients in the community. During the 1970s large-scale mental institutions were steadily discredited and there was a move away from the isolation of the mentally ill in old Victorian asylums towards their integration in the community. Locally the numbers of patients at Broadgate Hospital declined from about 450 in 1975 to about 250 in 1986. The East Yorkshire Health Authority faced a situation where it had two large institutions for the care of the mentally ill (Broadgate and De la Pole) both of which were operating at below-capacity and which were becoming more and more expensive to run. With the development of alternative residential care and community-based mental health teams (for example, Manor Road, Beverley) the Broadgate Hospital site became redundant.

Even before the last of Broadgates's patients left in April 1989 the site had been earmarked for residential development. This was the preferred option of the Yorkshire Regional Health Authority and had been recommended by a government inspector.

There is little doubt that the Broadgate site, so close to the visual splendour of Beverley's Westwood Pastures, was an attractive, and valuable, piece of real estate. Within two years of closure the bulk of the hospital buildings were gone to make way for scores of detached dwellings making up the Broadgate housing development. However, a remnant of the former buildings, the Ridings, remains as accommodation for the students of Bishop Burton College and as a reminder of its history in the care of the mentally ill.

24

The Capital of Caravan Making

One of the most important dates in the diaries of mobile home enthusiasts each year is the Caravan Extravaganza held at the Lawns site of Hull University in Cottingham. Eager to see the new touring models unveiled by manufacturers like Swift and Coachman and static holiday homes built by names like Willerby and Cosalt crowds of 20,000 or more flock to this annual event. East Yorkshire, as befits the capital of Britain's caravan manufacturing industry, also hosts a number of trade shows in September attracting buyers from all over Britain and Europe…

For over sixty years Hull and East Yorkshire has been at the centre of one of Britain's most dynamic industries: caravan manufacturing. However, those decades have also seen profound changes in the design of caravans and the organisation of the industry with the disappearance of some early pioneering names like Astral and the increasing importance of other players in the market like Swift Caravans.

The origins of caravan making in the area can be traced back to the austerity years at the end of the Second World War when local businessman, Walter Allan, identified a potential market for temporary holiday accommodation and founded Willerby Caravans (1944). It was he who began mass-producing small caravans with steel frames and canvas walls and by the mid-1950s had developed a touring caravan made from glass-reinforced plastic: the Willerby Vista. These days the focus of the company is on luxurious holiday homes like the New England; this looks more like a bungalow than a mobile home and is equipped with every modern convenience.

The early dominance of East Yorkshire in caravan manufacture owed much to the proximity of Hull docks through which the basic raw materials (like Scandinavian timber) could be imported and the finished products exported to markets like Holland and Belgium. Those who used wood and steel in their other enterprises quickly saw the opportunities that were available in the manufacture of caravans. One of these was the Spooner Group, a large timber and civil engineering firm who in 1959 launched Astral Caravans making both static holiday homes and tourers. Designs like the Travelite (an 11ft 6in touring caravan) were influenced by the Spooner's own enthusiasm for caravan holidays.

The success of Willerby and Astral in the booming caravan market helped to spawn a host of imitators as other individuals saw the potential for making their mark on the industry and rushed in with their own designs and innovations. One of these was Terry Reed who had been with Astral Caravans as a joiner but left in 1962 and with a capital of just £2,000 set up Ace Caravans at Colonial Street in Hull. Ace Caravans quickly established a reputation for quality and design and he was soon building five touring caravans a week for export to Holland. Thanks to innovations like a curved toughened-glass front window, an aluminium lower panel at the front of the caravan to absorb stone chips, a hand-operated water pump and fitted carpets the rise of Ace Caravans was meteoric. By the late 1960s Terry Reed had moved production to Swinemoor Lane in Beverley and in 1972 merged with another manufacturer, Belmont (who made holiday homes on an adjacent site) to form Ace Belmont International (ABI).

The Willerby Co. was founded in 1944 by Hull businessman Walter Allan. Shown here is the distinctive Vista model from the mid-1950s.

The continuing success of ABI was recognised by a Queen's Award for Export Achievement in 1988 and the company was floated on the stock market two years later. By 1998 ABI was employing 700 people at its Beverley site and was the country's biggest caravan manufacturer making famous brands like Ace, Marauder, Monza and Jubilee. However, caravan manufacture like any other industry dealing in luxuries is vulnerable to the ups and downs of the market and in March 1998 the company was forced into receivership with debts totalling more than £45 million. This together with over 400 redundancies was greeted with dismay in Beverley and although a buyer was found the difficulties of ABI led them to cease production of touring caravans altogether in 2001. These days the company specialises in the production of high quality holiday homes like the Colorado and the luxurious Westwood.

More consistently successful in the field of touring caravans has been the Swift Group based at Dunswell Road, Cottingham and which now owns many of Britain's most famous caravan brands including Abbey, Bessacarr, Sprite and Sterling. The story of Swift Caravans is a rags-to-riches affair since a company that in 2003 was making profits of over £10 million began life in 1964 as a small operation located in a garage on Hedon Road, Hull. The following year it was joined by Ken Smith and his wife Joan and a small team of versatile staff began building touring caravans with independent suspension, full insulation, eye-catching upholstery and fitted carpets. By 1966 there was also a thriving export market to West Germany with Swift Caravans adopting names like the Baronette, Alouette and Silhouette for their new models. The company moved to Cottingham in 1970 and since then has expanded its facilities with a training centre and a new factory complex.

Interior of the Swift Factory in Dunswell Road, Cottingham, showing the assembly of touring caravans.

Success in the caravan industry depends not only on the state of the economy but also on keeping up with new developments and with competitors. Back in the 1960s and 1970s caravans came with gas mantles for internal lighting, glass windows and hand or foot operated water pumps. In the twenty-first century items like acrylic double-glazing, mains electricity, showers and even air-conditioning are taken for granted by caravan enthusiasts.

The Swift Group is still a family-owned business (under the control of Peter Smith, the son of the founder) and has been able to foresee new developments and take advantage of the business opportunities they present. In 1986, for example, the first Swift motor homes were built and in December 1988 a new 28,000sq ft factory went into production to meet the demand; by 1990 the Swift Group were the United Kingdom's leading builder of coach-built motor homes. They have also been a major beneficiary of rationalisation in the caravan industry since many companies (like ABI) saw no future in touring caravans and sold their brands to the Swift Group. In this way Ace Caravans (sold by ABI to Swift in 2001) and a host of other famous brands are now manufactured at the Dunswell Road factory. The Swift Group now employs over 900 staff and holds at least a 35 per cent share of the market. However, even Swift are not immune to market forces and from time to time have had to make redundancies (for example, in 1991). As Tony Hailey, managing director of the Swift Group since May 1989, commented:

The size of the market for touring caravans is linked to the ups and downs of the economy. When the economy is in a period of growth we do well and when it is in recession we feel it because our market is very much for people who already own a touring caravan and want to trade up to a new one.

It is perhaps therefore not surprising that the Swift Group has continued to diversify as well as to modernise and since 2004 has been building holiday homes too. In the process they have created

A chance to compare caravans! The Lawns in Cottingham (on the outskirts of Hull) plays host each September to the Caravan Extravaganza.

100 new jobs at a factory on Hedon Road in Hull where the company had begun operations forty years earlier!

There is little doubt that September's Caravan Extravaganza (and other East Riding trade shows) are eagerly awaited by customers and manufacturers alike. Not only do they give the buying public the opportunity to see and compare the latest models in touring caravans and holiday homes but they also represent a major sales showcase for local firms like Atlas, Carnaby, Cosalt and Swift. Caravan shows are an important pointer to the future success of these companies and to the job security that depends on the orders generated.

25

Thomas Ferens and Hull

Over seventy years ago a wide new thoroughfare, Ferensway, was created through the centre of Hull clearing away a mass of slum housing. Planners of the time hoped that this visionary enterprise would become 'the north's premier street'. Unfortunately the outbreak of the Second World War and economic circumstances meant that the dreams of its creators have only recently begun to be realised. The forty-acre St Stephen's development to the west of Ferensway, which opened in 2007, was Hull's most exciting civil engineering project in modern times combining a transport interchange, a covered street, a shopping and leisure complex, a hotel and over 200 new homes. This Ferensway project was a fitting tribute to the vision of city planners of the inter-war years and also to the man the street was named after: Thomas Ferens, Hull's greatest benefactor...

The name Ferensway, chosen in 1931 for Hull's new arterial route through the city centre, was in honour of one of its greatest citizens who had died the previous year. Thomas Robinson Ferens however was not Hull-born; he was the son of George Ferens, a flour miller of New Shildon, County Durham and his early years were spent at school in Bishop Auckland and then, from the age of thirteen, as a clerk for the Stockton & Darlington Railway. From his subsequent meteoric rise to importance in Hull it is clear that Thomas Ferens was no ordinary clerk and from the start showed the traditional Victorian virtues of industry, thrift, sobriety and prudence. With a zeal for self-improvement he spent his evenings teaching himself grammar, arithmetic, mechanics and, most importantly, shorthand. In 1846 Isaac Pitman had published his first shorthand dictionary and at the age of twenty Ferens set out to master this new skill by writing down sermons in shorthand at his local chapel. Throughout his life Ferens was a devout Wesleyan Methodist and a strict teetotaller, attributes which the Hull industrialist and Quaker James Reckitt (himself a teetotaller) probably found appealing when Ferens applied for the job of his shorthand and confidential clerk in 1868. Reckitt & Sons was a firm manufacturing household products like starch, washing blue and black lead and in April 1868 Thomas Ferens, aged twenty-one, moved to his new job in Hull at a starting salary of £70 a year.

When Ferens joined Reckitts his duties included dealing with the handwritten correspondence of the firm, the analysis of the sales of its commercial travellers and the maintenance of a set of account books. His abilities and energy led to his rapid promotion, in just six years, to works' manager with a share in the profits. With the added incentive that the success of Reckitts would boost his own income he sought to improve productivity through closer monitoring of the workforce (with fines for lateness) and daily production targets. The story is told of a female worker who was asked by Ferens how many bags of washing blue she could tie in one minute; her performance then determined the daily target for the factory! To increase sales of Reckitts products Ferens also drew heavily on American strategies by concentrating on market research, strong brand names and heavy advertising. An astute businessman, Ferens realised the importance of being 'first' with new products and in relation to the launch of Robin Starch was to write: 'Before our competitors were awake we could make our position practically impregnable.'

Above left: Thomas Ferens (1847-1930) at about the age of twenty-one. He arrived in Hull in 1868 to work as confidential and shorthand clerk to James Reckitt at a salary of £70 a year.

Above right: Thomas Ferens made a major contribution to the success of Reckitt & Sons. Products like Robin Starch led to huge profits and when Reckitts became a public company in 1888 Ferens' shareholdings in it made him a rich man.

In 1888 Reckitts had become a public company and Ferens was a director accumulating personal wealth on a vast scale. By the 1920s his assets were worth, by his own estimation, £650,000 and his income was £30,000 a year at a time when the average weekly wage was less than £3. Where Ferens differed from others of his kind however was the use to which he put his vast wealth. Thomas Ferens, like his mentor James Reckitt, was a philanthropist and had no taste for personal luxury. He had always given freely to charity but in 1906, following his recovery from glaucoma, he began to give away his wealth on a much grander scale to numerous good causes, perhaps as a thanksgiving for the restoration of his health.

One of his first donations was that of land to the Young Peoples Institute, on Cottingham Road in Hull, as a recreation ground (1906) and he was closely involved in James Reckitt's scheme for a Garden Village, of better quality housing for working people, the following year. Other benefactions soon followed including land for a boating lake in East Park (1912), twelve almshouses (the Ferens Haven of Rest) on Holderness Road and the site of the Ferens Art Gallery in central Hull (opened 1927). Ferens had already shown himself to be a patron of the arts for he had been providing £1,000 a year since 1905 to buy paintings for the city's art collection. As befitting a shrewd businessman Ferens believed, when it came to giving, that it was important to 'keep the root and give the fruit' i.e. preserve the capital but spend the income it produced. Thus for the almshouses he built in

East Hull he undertook to provide £2,000 worth of Reckitts shares to support his bequest. The idea was that the income from these shares would pay indefinitely for the maintenance of the properties and the people who lived in them.

By the late 1920s Ferens was giving away over 80 per cent of his annual income of £30,000 to good causes but with typical modesty he spoke of donating huge sums as 'one of the greatest blessings of my life' and, reflecting his deeply religious outlook on life, wrote 'to God be all the praise for influencing me to do it.'

For Thomas Ferens a devotion to moral principles was the guiding tenet of his life and he fought hard for the things he believed in both as a member of the Brunswick Methodist church in Hull (where he and his wife taught Sunday school) and later as MP for East Hull from 1906 to 1918. At a time when drunkenness was a real problem in Victorian Hull Ferens was an active campaigner against the evils of alcohol. In 1880, for example, he encouraged the formation of a 'Temperance Club' for the workforce at Reckitts and in later life remained an active member of the National Temperance League. This strict morality however was also a factor in a family rift with his adopted son during the First World War; the latter had separated from his wife and Thomas Ferens believed his son had behaved badly.

Perhaps the greatest gift that Ferens gave to Hull came at the end of his life. He had long been a believer in the value of education as a means to self-improvement and had provided numerous

In February 1925 Ferens wrote to the lord mayor of Hull promising the sum of £250,000 in Reckitt's shares for the setting up of a university college in the city. He had already purchased a site in Cottingham Road, Hull for the purpose.

A portrait of Thomas Ferens
in 1913 by Sir Frank Dicksee.
(courtesy of the Guildhall
Collection, Hull City Council)

scholarships to Hull secondary schools. To kick-start higher education in the city he gave, in February 1925, £250,000 of Reckitts shares and sixty acres of land for the establishment of a university college in the city (subsequently Hull University). This gift, worth over £6 million at today's values, was both remarkable and generous and provided the foundation for the university's growth in the years following the Second World War.

Even before his death Ferens' diaries show the affection that the people of Hull had for him. On the occasion of his eightieth birthday, on the 5 May 1927, Hull school children were given a day's holiday and the bells of Holy Trinity church were rung in celebration. His death three years later was met with huge outpourings of grief for the people of Hull had lost an important champion. With his gifts to the city in excess of £1 million it is not surprising that a year later Hull's important new road, Ferensway, was named in honour of its greatest benefactor.

26

A Wealth of Acting Talent

The East Riding has long been associated with famous showbusiness names. Beginning after the Second World War celebrities like Brian Rix, Ian Carmichael, Tom Courtenay, John Alderton and Maureen Lipman have all helped to make the area a nursery of the acting profession…

Many people's first and only experience of acting takes place at a tender age when they 'perform' before proud parents at a nativity play or similar school event; few have the courage, opportunity or talent to make a success of the uncertain world of professional acting. Yet Hull and East Yorkshire was once home to a number of Britain's most celebrated stars and most enduring talents. Although a few came from wealthy or privileged backgrounds in the years before the Second World War, others had more humble origins.

Brian Rix is now in his eighties and better known these days as Lord Rix and president of MENCAP, the charity for the mentally handicapped. In these roles he has raised huge amounts of money for the charity and greatly increased public awareness of people with learning disabilities. Until his mid-1950s, however, Brian Rix was one of Britain's most respected comedy actors famous for 'losing his trousers' in numerous farces on stage and television. He was born in 1924 at Cottingham, near Hull, the son of a shipowner, but moved to the seaside town of Hornsea when he was four. After the Second World War he formed his own theatre company and was associated with the famous Whitehall Theatre in London as well as appearing in several film comedies including *The Night We Dropped a Clanger* (1959) and *Don't Just Lie There, Say Something* (1973).

Also born in the 1920s was the actor Ian Carmichael, whose father and three uncles developed a family optician's business into one of the area's most prestigious department stores, Carmichaels of Hull. From about the age of ten Ian lived at the village of Elloughton, west of Hull, but during term-time was a boarder at Scarborough College. Shortly before the Second World War he was awarded a place at the Royal Academy for Dramatic Arts although his acting career was effectively postponed until 1947 by military service. Like his contemporary, Brian Rix, Ian Carmichael had a flair for comedy although of a more subtle kind. In the 1950s he was a popular box-office star with a talent for playing well-meaning, if bumbling characters and naive innocents in a corrupt world. These acting abilities were shown well in a series of Boulting Brother's comedies like *Private's Progress* (1956) and he also starred alongside Peter Sellers in *I'm All Right Jack* (1959), a bitter satire about industrial relations of the time.

In the 1960s and 1970s Ian Carmichael developed a successful television career too playing 'upper-class types' like Bertie Wooster in a BBC series (1966-1967) based on the writings of P.G. Wodehouse and Lord Peter Wimsey in the mystery stories by Dorothy L. Sayers (1972-1975). His resilience as an actor is remarkable when you consider that at the age of eighty-three, long past normal retirement, he was playing the part of hospital secretary T.J. Middleditch in the ITV drama series *The Royal* set in his home county of Yorkshire!

The county has also seen acting talent nurtured among those from far less privileged backgrounds. Tom Courtenay was born in February 1937 into a typical working-class environment close to Hull's

Above left: Brian Rix was famous for 'losing his trousers' in farces at the Whitehall Theatre, London. (Image by Eric Grey, courtesy of Independent Film Producers Ltd)

Above right: Ian Carmichael's acting career spans over sixty years from the Boulting Brother's film comedies of the 1950s to ITV's hospital drama *The Royal* in 2003 where he played the part of hospital secretary T.J. Middleditch. (courtesy of Yorkshire Television/ITV Productions)

fish docks where his father was a ship's painter. Yet family encouragement, natural intelligence and a grammar-school education at the city's Kingston High School enabled the young Tom to rise above these humble origins and at the age of eighteen to leave for University College, London and a degree in English. The drudgery of working-class life in Hull's Hessle Road area in the period after the Second World War and his own struggles as a young actor in London were revealed years later in his book *Dear Tom: Letters from Home* (published in 2000). The book contained a collection of letters from his devoted mother Annie whose own literary potential had been thwarted by the typically low aspirations of working-class women in the Hull of that time.

From London University Tom went on to study at the Royal Academy of Dramatic Arts and in 1960 he joined the Old Vic. His rise to importance as an actor was meteoric and in 1962 he won a BAFTA for his starring role in the film *The Loneliness of the Long Distance Runner*. Tom Courtney's gaunt appearance and hard, angry eyes suited the kind of 'angry young man' movies in vogue in the early sixties. His ability to portray an innocent naivety also made him the natural choice for playing the character of *Billy Liar* (1963), a day-dreaming clerk at a firm of funeral directors who retreats into a world of deceit and make-believe. Another acting triumph came in 1965 with his role in David Lean's masterpiece *Dr Zhivago* for which he received an Oscar nomination. Despite this promising beginning his film career stalled in the 1970s mostly, due to his preference for the theatre. However, his brilliance as an actor was once more recognised in the 1983 film *The Dresser*, for which he received his second Oscar nomination and by the awarding of a knighthood in 2001.

About four years younger than Tom Courtenay was another boy with working-class roots: John Alderton. Although born at Gainsborough in Lincolnshire the family moved to Hull where his parents were greengrocers. Like Tom Courtney before him, John Alderton too was a pupil at Kingston High

School and received his earliest training in school plays. By the age of eighteen he was planning to go to university to become an architect but was persuaded by a friend to audition for RADA instead.

In 1961 the twenty-one-year-old professional actor made his first appearance on stage in a play called *Badger's Green* at the Theatre Royal, York. In the same year he became familiar to television viewers in the early ITV soap opera *Emergency Ward 10* playing the part of Dr Moone. It was however as the naive but idealistic school teacher Bernard Hedges in the London Weekend Television comedy *Please Sir* that many will remember him. This popular programme ran for four years between 1968 and 1972 and Alderton also reprised the role of the hapless schoolteacher in the film version released in 1971. In fact the 1970s were the boom years of John Alderton's television career. In 1972 he appeared in the situation comedy *My Wife Next Door* and in 1974-1975 with his wife Pauline Collins in the groundbreaking domestic comedy *No Honestly*. The two went on to star together in other memorable drama series like *Upstairs Downstairs*, its spin-off *Thomas and Sarah*, and *Forever Green*, a series first shown in 1989 about town folk turned country bumpkins.

John Alderton has been married to Pauline Collins for thirty-eight years and they have one of the strongest marriages in show business. Their daughter Kate is also an actress and the three appeared together on stage in 2004 in a successful run of the play *Going Straight*, the story of two old gangsters settling into the quiet life of retirement!

In fact John's own semi-retirement had been interrupted the previous year when he had been persuaded by wife Pauline to take a part in the acclaimed film drama *Calendar Girls*. Filmed in the beautiful Yorkshire Dales he played the part of a man dying of leukaemia who becomes the inspiration for a nude calendar of Women's Institute members seeking to raise money for research into the illness. In fact *Calendar Girls* was not John Alderton's first movie experience in Yorkshire; back in 1976 he had played the part of the county's most famous veterinary surgeon, James Herriot, in the film *It Shouldn't Happen to a Vet*.

The Aldertons together! John Alderton, his wife Pauline Collins and his daughter Kate Alderton working together in the stage play *Going Straight* in 2004. (courtesy of Bill Kenwright Ltd)

Above left: Maureen Lipman in the stage play *Martha, Josie and Chinese Elvis.* (Image by Robert Day, courtesy of the Theatre Royal Windsor)

Above right: Liam Garrigan is one of East Yorkshire's 'new generation' of acting talent. A former student of the Northern Theatre in Hull, Liam has appeared in the hospital drama *Holby City* and more recently in the BBC drama series *The Chase.* (courtesy of Liam Garrigan)

Another of Hull's enduring stars is the actress Maureen Lipman who will be remembered by many as the Jewish grandmother in the British Telecom television advertisements of the 1980s. Probably her most famous line in playing the comedy part was in conversation with her dispirited grandson Anthony about his poor exam results. After hearing he had passed sociology came the classic comment: 'an ology! He gets an ology and he says he's failed. You get an ology, you're a scientist!'

Maureen Lipman was born in 1946 and was the daughter of a Jewish tailor. Educated at Hull's Newland High School she was pressured into acting by her mother Zelda who took her to the pantomime and pushed her onto the stage. After training at the London Academy of Music and Dramatic Art she landed the role of Sylvie in the film *Up the Junction* alongside Dennis Waterman (1967). Her career never looked back and in the forty years she has been in the acting profession she has rarely been out of work.

A star of the stage, film and television one of her memorable performances was that of Trish in the film *Educating Rita* (1983) for which she won an award for best-supporting actress. She has also appeared on stage and television in her one-woman show about her favourite comedy heroine Joyce Grenfell and has also taken parts in some of British television's most famous programmes of recent years including *Coronation Street, Jonathan Creek* and *Dr Who.*

The story of Maureen Lipman and the rest is a clear indication of the part the county has played, and continues to play, in the development of the performing arts. Since 1975 the Northern Theatre School in Hull (now the Northern Academy of Performing Arts) has been at the forefront of training future thespians and its talented students have included Paul Popplewell and Liam Garrigan, now renowned actors in their own right. With its vibrant local theatre scene it seems likely that East Yorkshire will be creating many fine actors into the future.

Other local titles published by The History Press

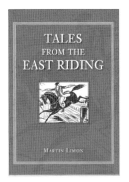

Tales From The East Riding
MARTIN LIMON

The old East Riding of Yorkshire has had a rich and varied past and Martin Limon's historical collection features some of the people, places and events that have made it that way. Here are tales of pygmies and giants, Roman villas and Victorian workhouses, famous industrialists and infamous highwaymen, all with a place in the county's history.

978 07524 4038 5

Olde Yorkshire Punishments
HOWARD PEACH

This fascinating volume explores the darkest aspects of crime and punishment in Yorkshire over the centuries – a history by turns gruesome, intriguing and strange. From the stocks, joug and branding iron to the prison cell, galley – and noose – every punishment that could befall the criminals of Yorkshire is included in this volume. With sections on Church scandals, why bull baiting was a legal requirement and the use of the Sharp Maiden – the guillotine – it will delight anyone with an interest in Yorkshire's history.

978 07524 4661 5

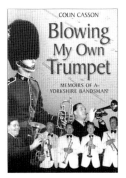

Blowing My Own Trumpet: Memoirs of a Yorkshire Bandsman
COLIN CASSON

From memories of childhood and early days in the Black Dyke Mills to trooping the colour with the Irish Guard and his debut with Geraldo, this charming collection of tales from Haworth musician Colin Casson takes the reader from Westminster Abbey to Northern Ireland, Europe, Australia – and the Hollywood of the 1950s. This warm, witty and distinctly down-to-earth story of one musician's life will delight music lovers everywhere.

978 07524 4719 3

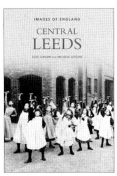

Central Leeds
ROSE GIBSON AND MICHELE LEFEVRE

This impressive selection of over 200 old photographs and illustrations whisks the reader away on an exciting and informative tour of central Leeds as it used to be. Explore the changing face of City Square and other central landmarks, and meet some of the characters – such as the renowned Throp brothers – who helped shape their development.
 Spanning well over 100 years, these images – drawn primarily from the library's extensive photo archive – provide a unique insight into a way of life now lost.
978 07524 4005 7

If you are interested in purchasing other books published by The History Press, or in case you have difficulty finding any History Press books in your local bookshop, you can also place orders directly through our website

www.thehistorypress.co.uk